Enough with the Secrets, Mama!

ENOUGH WITH THE SECRETS, MAMA!

An Immigrant Woman's Story of Overcoming Failure,
Equipping Women with the Skills Needed to
Enjoy a Fruitful Life Free of Maternal Heartache

LIN GREEN

NEW YORK

LONDON • NASHVILLE • MELBOURNE • VANCOUVER

Enough with the Secrets, Mama!

An Immigrant Woman's Story of Overcoming Failure, Equipping Women with the Skills Needed to Enjoy a Fruitful Life Free of Maternal Heartache

© 2024 Lin Green

Published in New York, New York, by Morgan James Publishing. Morgan James is a trademark of Morgan James, LLC. www.MorganJamesPublishing.com

Proudly distributed by Publishers Group West®

Unless otherwise marked, Scripture taken from the HOLY BIBLE, NEW LIVING TRANSLATION, Copyright© 1996, 2004, 2007 by Tyndale House Foundation. Used by permission of Tyndale House.

Scripture quotations marked MSG are taken from THE MESSAGE, copyright © 1993, 2002, 2018 by Eugene H. Peterson. Used by permission of NavPress, represented by Tyndale House Publishers. All rights reserved

Morgan James BOGO™

A **FREE** ebook edition is available for you or a friend with the purchase of this print book.

CLEARLY SIGN YOUR NAME ABOVE

Instructions to claim your free ebook edition:
1. Visit MorganJamesBOGO.com
2. Sign your name CLEARLY in the space above
3. Complete the form and submit a photo of this entire page
4. You or your friend can download the ebook to your preferred device

ISBN 9781636982861 paperback
ISBN 9781636982878 ebook
Library of Congress Control Number: 2023944060

Cover Design by:
Rachel Lopez
www.r2cdesign.com

Interior Design by:
Christopher Kirk
www.GFSstudio.com

Morgan James PUBLISHING **Builds** with... **Habitat for Humanity®** Peninsula and Greater Williamsburg

Morgan James is a proud partner of Habitat for Humanity Peninsula and Greater Williamsburg. Partners in building since 2006.

Get involved today! Visit: www.morgan-james-publishing.com/giving-back

*To my elementary school English teacher, Mrs. Lila K. Mullins,
who inspired my love of the English language,
its words, and everything it represents.
Because of you, I've been able to dream past the realities I've
faced and was transported to a new dimension
that has engulfed me forever. Thank you for believing in me.
Rest in heaven.*

TABLE OF CONTENTS

FOREWORD

If there is one book that can change your life, you're holding it in your hand. *Enough with the Secrets, Mama!* has the potential to transform your life. I believe this book is one of the most important and timely messages you will ever read. This book is not only transparent and relevant, but it is revolutionary and healing.

> *Sometimes God redeems your story by surrounding*
> *you with people who need to hear your past,*
> *so it doesn't become their future.*
> John Acuff

I have lived the above quote over the past twelve years, after having buried my pain and secrets not only brought me into a deep state of depression, but also thoughts of taking my own life. Never a good idea. We bury our secrets with our shame, and *hope* seems so very distant. But God has a way of turning our deepest pain into our greatest purpose.

Now my purpose is greater than ever, and hope is stronger than ever and so is my wisdom. The past eleven years have taught me a great principle, "I will never trust a man without a limp." It is difficult to hear or take the advice of people who never show you their limp. They never share their vulnerability or brokenness, wearing masks believing we can't see the fake.

If the Bible was written by perfect people, not one of us could relate to it. That's why God chose broken men and women, whom He redeemed to show us His grace and redemption in our story.

I have had the honor to be Lin's pastor and friend for many years. I have personally watched the Lord touch and heal her life into who she has become today. This is but still the beginning. This Scripture has always been a gentle reminder of what God can do when we open the book of our hearts to His eyes, He will invade it with purpose. We become wounded healers to the broken.

God made my life complete when I placed all the pieces before him. When I cleaned up my act, he gave me a fresh start. Indeed, I've kept alert to God's ways; I haven't taken God for granted. Every day I review the ways he works, I try not to miss a trick. I feel put back together, and I'm watching my step. God rewrote the text of my life when I opened the book of my heart to his eyes.
                                         2 Samuel 22:21–25, MSG

"Appreciate failure as the stepping-stone to greatness." (Lin Green) Her words will change your life because they are true.

Lin's message, *Enough with the Secrets, Mama!,* is an invitation to let go and let God begin to heal your life. The book will challenge and encourage you to take a step beyond living with secrets and start living for a bigger purpose.

Are you ready to begin the greatest journey of your life? Now, let the journey begin because your life is about to change!

Lin, I am so proud of what God has done in your life, and I am honored to add my name as one who will hold your arms up in this life.

-Sam Hinn, senior pastor, The Gathering Place

Chapter 1
HUMBLE BEGINNINGS

Ever wonder what your parent's life was like before you came along? Like truly, honestly considered their lives as adults and their pressures, their concerns, their responsibilities, their dreams, and their aspirations? It wasn't until my son reached the age of maturity that I began to think about this myself.

Over the last several years, I took a step back and did a lot of self-evaluation. During this time, I began to consider these things. What I knew about my parents is what most of us know growing up. They cared for me; they worked; they provided in the best way they knew how; they instilled certain values and morals, and they led us on the way to adulthood. As the years passed, I would learn more than I had ever imagined about my mother and father, but specifically my maternal example. I learned things that would explain why she became the woman she is today. I'd learn how she developed the very characteristics that our family not only admires, but even considers, and at what cost? My biological father? Or whom I so lovingly describe as my sponsor—well, I know very little about him. I know only what I've been told over the years by his other children and family members. My mother was careful not to muddy his image as she would later express in my adulthood. It wasn't her place.

My mother comes from a large family comprising eleven children, some of which were born to both my grandmother and grandfather. And others were born out of wedlock (as I've been told). If you're a minority family, you learn later on in life the many family 'secrets' that have been carried over the years. In fact, whether you're a minority or not, we've likely all experienced the same. There are things that are never spoken about, things swept under the rug for one reason or another. Whether it be to save the family name or avoid discord. But did it really avoid discord? There's a lot of familial animosity that exists within our tree. Moments of tit for tat. Sibling rivalries. Stories heard by some one way and interpreted by some in another. I've learned the animosity carried on through my family comes from deep within the familial structure stemming from events that occurred long before we were ever a thought in the mind of our Creator. The one and only, G-O-D. And it is this very thread of experiences that creates the genetic makeup for what would follow with their offspring—their descendants, namely my cousins, my siblings, and myself. Some call it a generational curse. I call it a generational cycle. A cycle that caused a lot of avoidance and failure to discuss things as if they were non-existent. Family "unknowns" that would creep back up decades to follow. If you're reading this and find similarities in your familial relationships and upbringing, it's no coincidence.

Challenges within one's family structure are one thing. But facing these challenges, coupled with the ones in a developing country, is vastly different than facing them in a nation of independence and opportunity. It's a dog-eat-dog world, thus creating a strong-willed, independent thinker like my mother. One who would stand up for what was right (often fighting off bullies for her siblings at school). She would get lost in the reality of what it meant to take a stand in circumstances where she would otherwise be seen as less than, incapable, or not worthy. She braved it, nonetheless. The courage was truly admirable. It created a woman her siblings looked up to. There being an exception to the rule, I'm certain there may have been sibling rivalries among those eleven children at some point. It's only natural. These were among the few challenges that forged a woman destined for career freedom. Seeking an outward expression of creativity, she revealed her love for beauty and fashion. *The history of beauty and fashion details the artistic form of escaping the status quo.*[1] She would soon have the liberty of expressing this side of her when she met her first husband at the tender age of sixteen.

––––––

Prior to meeting and marrying *our sponsor*, my mother wed a successful businessman. A man who would father their first-born son. She lived the life of a *high-ranking* wife along with this businessman. He took care of her, and she, in turn, took care of her family (parents and siblings included). But she was no stranger to this role. Caring for others came naturally to her, sometimes to a fault. Whether out of responsibility, expectation, or concern, she gladly asserted herself in this role. She was the lead carrier of the freedom flag in the family. Not only did my mother have the means, but she also had the position to assist some of her siblings in seeking the same freedom in "the States." She would go on to support them in any way she could with the legal resident application process and may have even contributed financially to the cause. No family member was left behind.

As pure as the intentions may have been, these luxuries afforded to her would later lead to the falling out of some relationships, including the struggling and troubled relationship she initiated with her son in the years to come. Expectations were at an all-time high, and let's just say, sometimes they were too high. My mother expected the best from her family. After all, in her eyes, she made some major sacrifices. She had looked out for them. It was in this space of grandiosity that her sibling relationships began to fail. Some may have even considered that she was "losing herself" in the process. To ask them their opinion would mean you're going to hear numerous variations of the same circumstance, opening up a Pandora's Box of endless disagreements.

If you knew my mother then, you'd know she was the apple of her father's eye. The child that could do no wrong, and she reveled in this fact. It made her feel grand. It confirmed her self-esteem. This encouraged the "I can have anything I set my mind to" mentality. After all, what every young lady wants to feel in her upbringing is a sense of pride. That pride was reciprocal between father and daughter. That bond was seen as "favor" by her siblings. Yet she and her father both knew how special it was. My mother catered to her dad, looking after him when he arrived home, and making sure he felt loved and cared for. A love separate and apart from that of my grandmother, his wife. This was a daddy-daughter kind of love, which made it all the easier for her to seek love in adulthood. She was confident; with her head held high, she could conquer anything. The world was at her feet. And with this sense of confidence, she would attract a man that had similar characteristics. A man that was strong-willed, focused, and loved his family. The continuum of this grandiose nature would follow her throughout her life. She married this man, the father of her firstborn child. The first for both of them. His namesake.

This husband of hers was a proud father. He often took my brother along to meetings, sometimes to strip clubs, and often to bars. As a young boy, he was exposed to more than he should have been. It wouldn't be long before he would live a life that would lead him to early alcohol use—and further lead him to troubling encounters with substances. It was as if a pattern she ignored in her childhood was now rearing its ugly head. Unknowingly, she too was creating a child with a grandiose personality. However, one who took self-esteem to another level. An unkind level. Self-esteem far surpassing his own imagination. As some would say, he'd soon grow to be too big for his britches. His attitude grew out of control. It was the opposite effect that the powerful environment had on her, in fact. It humbled her in some ways, often incorporating the well-being of others into her day-to-day thoughts and concerns. While my brother, on the other hand, was developing a more self-entitled, selfish attitude. It was all about him and there's nothing anyone could say to the contrary.

When I think of the 1980s, these are the things to which I am prone to connect. As a lover of history, religion, and the arts, I can visualize this time being one of many accomplishments and many failures for the world at large. In the United States, there were a series of events that were pivotal. Specifically, in May 1981 (the year I was born), the following occurred:

May 1981 USA

Jerry Seinfeld was born to comedy this month, performing for his 1st national audience. (5/7)

Pope John Paul II was shot and seriously wounded by a Turkish Gunman. (5/13)

The first news article about AIDS appeared in the newspaper, New York Native. (5/18)

Ronald Reagan became the oldest man to serve as President of the United States, at age seventy and 109 days (5/26)[2]

I look back on the eighties, however, with a different sense of appreciation for the life my loving mother experienced. While more relevant to my mother at that time, it was a year when the Dominican Women Feminist movement took flight after the unfortunate slaying of the Mirabal sisters in 1961, in the wake of the dictatorship at the hands of then President Trujillo. The organizing of women, from the late 1970s and early 1980s, to create inclusive groups focused on consciousness-raising was a core goal of the growing feminist movement across the region.[3]

Inclusion; let's talk about that. In this movement, as in the life of my mother, it was important to have stability. To be an inclusive part of history that was empowering. The feeling of empowerment that drove her to succeed. There was a sense of peace and strength she had in this space. Her every move had a purpose, strategically mapping out her goals and putting one foot in front of the other with a predetermined plan. The overall goal was never to give up, never to give in, and to give it all she had to ultimately make her mark. It was important for her to continue to uphold this leadership role. Now, more than ever, she had to maintain a sense of dignity in the process. Though she didn't account for any hiccups along the way, you'd surely think she did, but she just kept on rolling. Disillusioned or not, nothing would stop her from reaching her destination.

Now divorced from her previous husband, and continuously looking for progress, it was no surprise that my mother sought some independent liberties in her career as an entrepreneur and beautician in Puerto Rico, where she would soon meet my biological father. It wasn't uncommon during this time for many Dominican natives to seek opportunity in what was, at that time, the closest and most popular place to seek freedom. My brother, however, stayed behind in the Dominican Republic during this time.

Although there were substantial upper-class and middle-class segments in the Dominican Republic, the country was also experiencing a high poverty rate. Since the 1970s, the poor economy of the Dominican Republic had rampantly driven emigration. Though many Dominicans who moved to Puerto Rico stayed and started a life there, some Dominicans (and even other Latinos/people of Caribbean descent like Haitians and Cubans) used it as a temporary stopping point to the US mainland.

What a perfect opportunity for those looking to escape the harsh realities of financial struggle in the Dominican Republic, my mother included. After all, her circumstances had changed remember? She was accustomed to a life of "privilege," and she quite enjoyed it. I mean, who wouldn't? And so did her family. Reaping the benefits of the financial freedoms of her ex-husband—and all the perks that came with it—was the icing on the proverbial cake. She didn't want to leave that behind. The financial stability, that is. She began to drum up ways to accomplish that on her own. Her beauty business was taking off. Her salon opening and the success of said business led her to consider opportunities abroad. It was known that "the states" offered numerous opportunities to learn the up-and-coming trends in the beauty industry and she wasn't going to get left behind. Ahead of her time, she was constantly forward-thinking.

My mother's business was thriving, and she had seen her efforts at gaining more knowledge of the industry by obtaining an Alien Registration Visa which allowed her to travel to beauty conferences in New York. Independence was always at the forefront of her mind. It was during this time that she would meet my *"sponsor."*[4]

Fast forward to mid-May 1981, just a year and a half after the birth of my mother's first-born daughter (whom she struggled to conceive after a seventeen-year stint of trying) I came along. In fact, by now, my mother had solidified her role as the lead sibling in the family. The one to seek freedoms and opportunities and, in the essence of Hispanic cultural responsibility, help her family along. Becoming the godmother to nieces and nephews and bringing home luxuries they otherwise wouldn't have been afforded. Clothes she had purchased in her travels abroad, things that they had not yet seen or experienced. Often even having clothes custom-tailored for herself and others. She was the poster child for setting your mind to do the very things you set forth to accomplish.

But life isn't all it's cracked up to be, you see. A relationship that others would view as flourishing would soon take a turn for the worse. As in many troubled relationships—initially, the signs weren't as clear. Though there may be a number of "red flag" moments exhibited at the start of a new relationship, your emotional capacity to consider those as red flags when you are young and in love is less likely. In fact, you may consider comments about your appearance, controlling behaviors, and verbal disagreements, leading to emotional outbursts as "yellow flags," even though one too many of these kinds of incidents can lead to a tumultuous relationship. The controlling nature becomes less verbal and more physical, and so the cycle of violence begins. Once full of life, my mother's light began to dwindle.

Chapter 2

DARKNESS FALLS

As if a dark cloud filled the skies above her, she began to incur complications in this new life. Without having been privy to much information, I later confirmed that during this point in her relationship with our *sponsor,* she was starting to see signs of more serious trouble. It wasn't what she expected it would be. The honeymoon period quickly faded away, and darkness fell upon her. There she was, eight months pregnant with me, and loads of thoughts were flashing through her mind. *What am I doing? Can I continue to live this way? How is this going to affect my unborn child?* A multitude of things would occupy her mental space. Not only was she contemplating the daily struggles she faced, but she also started having pregnancy complications. Could it have been the stress she was enduring?

As a fetus, I was troubling. My fetal gestation movement was slim to none. In other words, there was little to no activity in my mother's womb. Doctors quickly alerted her that something wasn't right. This information led to talks of her need to consider a legal abortion. A medical procedure ruled I wasn't going to be a "fit" infant. I was going to have some deficiencies, they said. Something was critically wrong, as the lack of movement proved I was not fit to be carried for much longer. Or was I? Alternately, they gave her the option of getting an amniocentesis, which is a procedure used to take out a small sample of the amniotic fluid for testing. This would allow them to check for chromosomal abnormalities.

I've heard this is a painful procedure but, in the spirit of a true mother's love, she agreed to endure it. Anything to "save the fetus" is what she said. And she refused to have an abortion. Test results returned revealing that I was going to do just fine, and she could breathe a sigh of relief. Doctors concluded that I was simply just comfortable in my fetal position. No need to move, as I had found quite the perfect spot. Funny how this would become the *expectant ideology* of my life.

So there we were, my sister and me. We share the same biological footprint, both deriving from a Puerto Rican sponsor and a Dominican Matriarch. My mother's success in business allowed us to experience an "easier" way of life. Yes, this meant that as kids, we had a privileged upbringing. My mother wouldn't have had it any other way. It meant that we had luxuries afforded to us that came with a certain upbringing. A nanny, a cook, someone who tidied up the house, and the ability to witness it all in her presence. I recall bits and pieces of this time in my childhood. The memories that stick with me the most today consist of days in the salon where I weaseled my way into trouble. Days that involved climbing on salon chairs and taking it upon myself to use the scissors and cut a sleeping senior patron's hair as he waited his turn for a haircut.

I held conversations with clients using the few choice words I knew as a toddler, repeating things I had heard my mother say. Some, not so appropriate, might I add. However, I recall the laughs from the patrons who were both shocked and amused by my use of those very words, and this filled me with joy. So I did it over and over again. I also recall tender moments with my nanny as she rocked me to sleep. The movement I've since adopted as part of my nightly sleeping ritual. Nostalgically, I rock myself to sleep as an adult, swaying my feet back and forth, causing my bottom to rock in the same manner I'd been put to sleep as a toddler. These make up some of my exceedingly fond memories.

By the time I was two years old, the honeymoon period between my parents had long passed. I would later learn that things became quite volatile. Though I don't recall much, if any of it, my mother later explained that she "left" one night after having had enough. Having already sketched out a plan, she packed our belongings and stashed them away secretly where our father wouldn't find them. And after he returned home from a drunken night out, a heated exchange ensued between them, which led to threatening her with a firearm. Needless to say, she did what any desperate mother would do in that instance. She feigned resistance, buttered him up, and encouraged him to return to the "bar" or wherever he came from. This was the perfect opportunity to make a run for it. And so she did. The events that immediately followed are a blur. Let's just say, childhood amnesia was a blessing.[5] Also called infantile amnesia, this is the inability of adults to retrieve episodic memories (memories of situations or events) before the age of two to four years old.[6]

My mind flashes back to one warm moment during this tumultuous time, however. I remember my older sister and I were dressed in our jean pants, shiny white custom shoes (I was born pigeon-toed and required the adjustment), and Menudo T-shirts. For those who don't know, this Menudo tee was a big deal. Menudo was none other than the biggest of the Latin boy bands in history, especially during this time. Off we went, happy and trotting along, ready for the adventure. Not understanding the totality of what was happening, to us, it was an adventure! And almost as if to capture the innocence and joy of that moment, my mother photographed us while we explored the airport. Pictures that depicted how eager we were to travel into the unknown. I remember the sound of the *tip-tapping* of our feet, running along into the bright hangar where we boarded a flight back to the Dominican Republic.

Chapter 3

DOMINICAN ROOTS

And so we began a new life, back to my mother's roots—back to her home and place of comfort. We spent a lot of time with my grandparents during our time there. I have vague memories of time spent with our grandparents in Santo Domingo, Dominican Republic in this brief stint. It was during this time that my mother initiated our preparation for a *"better life."* She tried to establish some custodial responsibility for our sponsor and made efforts to hold our father accountable for his role in supporting us financially by establishing a child support order through their divorce process. This was yet another one of those pieces of memorabilia I would find in a suitcase filled with old photos growing up. The curious kid that I was, I examined this piece of 3x5-inch notecard as if to make sense of what happened to be little documented dates for payments received. The total balance received is among the many things I recall. I remember seeing this and thinking,

'This couldn't possibly be enough to take care of us.' I can't imagine having to raise two children on the shortchange he was providing. Knowing my mother, I know she initiated this out of principle. She wasn't going to subject herself to such ridicule, since to her, it seemed he was being spiteful by withholding funds. But I digress.

In the true spirit of love, she found herself reconnecting with a long-lost love during this time. He, as I'm told by familial sources, was enamored by my mother, and the feeling was mutual. Reconnecting was only natural after so many years. He was sharp; a staple in the political party of that time, providing secret service duty for the then Dominican president. Tall, dark, handsome, and intelligent. He, too, had recently gotten divorced. Having had children from his previous marriage as well, it was fate that they would meet again. It was seemingly a fresh start for both of them. Finding their way back to each other again. This man would become the only male role model we would ever have. Herein referred to as *my father* because stepdad is just too grand a demotion for a man who raised us as if we were his own.

While working in politics, my father was subject to the political instability and the civil unrest of the people. Assassinations of party representatives weren't uncommon. Revolutions, revolts, insurrections, and social and political breakdowns were all common threads in the political system of this third-world country. It was this very thread of violence that would soon force my father to flee the country and seek refuge in the United States. Facts I would only learn after discovering a book in my parents' bedroom with his picture in it. More of this major revelation to follow in the pages to come.

To be honest, that period of transition while living in Santo Domingo is nearly absent from my childhood memory. Possibly because, shortly after, we embarked on another adventure. This time, we were heading to the land of freedom and opportunity. We landed in the United States, specifically Providence, Rhode Island after being in DR for two years. Here we started a new life, alongside our father. He was the only father we would ever know, for our *sponsor* was never again to be seen. Though our sponsor knew where we were, he simply didn't take the steps to come to see about us. I recall seeing my paternal aunt often during these times. She would visit us in Providence frequently, always eager to spend time with us and shower us with her love. She was extremely fond of her nieces. These were among the happiest memories of our early years in Providence. But it wouldn't be long before this gradually shifted to more troubling times as the return of my brother was both a gift and a curse.

Although uncertain of the logistical preparations it took to get him from the Dominican Republic to Providence, Rhode Island, it was still nice to have him around. It was a familiarity in a new place we didn't know we needed. As kids, he did his share of looking after us. Taking great care of his little sisters was an honor for him. Likely, the few times he would experience great joy in his life. Knowing that he had us to look up to him, but that wouldn't last long. After a while, he started disappearing for days and weeks on end, returning home with a stench of alcohol and the smell of the streets. Under the influence, some days, and bruised and battered other days. Sadly, he had clearly climbed the ranks of alcoholism and substance abuse.

Our loving and quiet new home soon went from light and airy to dark and gloomy. My mother's moods were clearly affected. She was dull and low-spirited, worried, and anxious all the time. The responsibilities that rested on her shoulders were pivotal to the smooth transition in this new place we now called home. On top of making sure we were enrolled in school, she now had the unfortunate job of keeping a close eye on my brother. Tears and anguish were a norm in her series of emotional expressions. I recall times he'd disappear longer than usual, and I remember visiting hospital emergency rooms with the last speck of hope of finding him, only to return home and see him stumbling down the block toward our three-story multi-family home. As we watched with care and concern, he walked up to the front porch, sometimes stumbling in his steps. We sat in the car in awe of the pain, the constant state of disconcertedness in which my mother lived. It would be years before she'd have some "relief."

By the time I was five years old, I was eager to learn the English language, since Spanish was the primary language spoken in our home. My sister started school before I did in 1984. As she walked up the narrow steps of the yellow school bus in front of our home, I watched eagerly from the rust-orange steps of our front porch. When she'd returned, I was the eager little sister who wanted to listen in on this "gibberish" she was speaking. Or at least that is what it sounded like to me at the time. I tuned into *Sesame Street* during this time, where I got a head start on learning these words my sister was spewing so easily. Being able to connect with the Latino characters portrayed on the show was pivotal to my developmental growth. The *Sesame Street* Season 16 cast would become a staple in our home.

Our days were filled with childlike wonder during that period of our childhood. We especially enjoyed the simple pleasures of outside life. A tomboy at heart, I spent ample time outside with my friends. Playing with marbles in the dirt, jumping from garage to garage as our backyards were lined with garages that spanned the length of the entire block. Some garages were abandoned with roofs nearly caving in. In these garages, we sought refuge from childlike responsibilities such as chores. We played hide and seek, rode our bikes, and, in the summer months when the heat was unbearable, we pulled out the water hoses and ran through the bursting fire hydrants. This . . . was . . . joy! A simpler time. But it wouldn't be without its share of turmoil. See, as we were frolicking in our own childlike wonder, in the distance lay the very things that were determined to steal our joy.

It was during this time that my innocence was stolen. My spirit zapped from right in front of me. All because of a tall, fair-skinned, slick-haired, dorky pervert who swept in and invaded the parts of me that I considered sacred. Cornering me in stairways as I made my way into my home or the homes of my neighborhood friends. He'd eagerly watch my every move like a hawk, looking for the next opportunity to fondle me, forcefully placing his sloppy wet lips on mine as I cringed and tried pulling back, only causing him to force all the more.

His threats to "out me" as the one initiating these acts only made me shrivel up in fear. He claimed he'd turn my story around on me as if I was the perverted one seeking his attention. *Could he do that?* I thought This supposed family friend and neighbor was the first of four accounts in my childhood in which I'd lose just a bit more of my cheerfulness. I remember feeling helpless, frozen, and afraid. I was unprotected and alone. Ashamed that I kept finding myself in this position over and over. Like, how could I be so careless as to not notice his whereabouts and avoid them? If you can believe it, I blamed myself a lot. My light dimmed more and more with each account that robbed me of childhood enjoyment. I recall having various nightmares during this time. Dreams so vivid, I awoke in a dazed and confused state of mind. Imagine feeling this way at a time where you should be waking up cheerful and with reckless abandon. My lack of innocence would turn into a need for constant control of my environment. There was a sense of guilt that followed me into my adolescence. The need to make the world around me as perfect and peaceful as possible because, well, it was so imperfect and unpeaceful within me. Or so I tried, by any means necessary, to make it that way because failure was not an option.

Oblivious to the world around me, because of all that was happening to me, I later learned that my brother fathered a child with an older woman during this time. This woman was also heavily involved in his same lifestyle. So it was no surprise that this child, my niece and soon-to-be "little sister," would be removed from the mother as were her previous children, and such was the destiny of most of the children that came after. My mother would have it no other way than to take my "little sister" in and raise her as her own, giving her the life she otherwise wouldn't have had in the hands of her negligent parents.

Here we were, now a family of five. My father, mother, and sisters are all under one roof. Suffering silently, my mother dealt with my brother's continued addiction. For her, there were many sleepless nights. Nights I can now see she likely cried herself to sleep, turning in anguish as she worried about his whereabouts and his wellbeing. Some days when he disappeared for longer than she was able to withstand, she piled my older sister and me in the car and we visited hospital emergency rooms. Holding on to hope as we walked in with her translating her words to the hospital staff, inquiring whether he had been admitted. Refer to the previously mentioned account of seeing him walking nonchalantly back home, as this would happen quite often. Too many times to count, in fact. His head held down as he made his way up the block and past us, walking into the home as our eyes followed and we knew better than to say a word. Knowing the turn of events would be both heart-wrenching and exciting as my mother saw him finally come home. It was a mix of emotions.

There were many talks of rehabilitation, followed by heated discussions, which ultimately led to him walking back out. Starting the anguish-filled days all over again until we either heard from him or saw him. But who would've known this next time would be different? The call came from a correctional facility with news we were never expecting. It seems he got caught in a trap of sorts. Accompanied by some so-called friends, he answered a knock at the door of an apartment where he was staying. And there, standing at the door, was an undercover Drug Enforcement Administration agent. He unknowingly sold this agent some drugs, and well . . . the rest is history. The next time we saw him, he was dressed in all denim at the Boston Federal Correctional Facility. He was held there for months, awaiting his sentencing and deportation. We visited him at least once a month. My mother brought him the personal items he'd requested in an effort to make his "stay" more comfortable. Maybe, in some way, because it was also what she was used to—taking care of him. Even though, at this moment, it really didn't matter. Our little sister, his daughter, was told he was in "school" each time we visited. We later found out that she was well aware of the place where he was being held. And the joke was on us. But she went along with it. She was always such a smart little girl. Though, she had never spent much time with him. He was too engulfed in his own world to even consider parenting at the time. Luckily, she had all she needed in us. She was loved to no end. Spoiled even, but my mother wouldn't have it any other way. It's as if she was the piece of him she was unable to hold on to.

Chapter 4

CHANGE OF PACE

It wasn't long before my brother was officially deported. Extradited back to the very country that raised him. The place that was responsible for his love of the streets, where he created this persona that cared only for himself. I must have been twelve years old then, and by this time we were no longer living in that three-story multi-family home in Rhode Island. My mother had been approved for Section 8 housing in the projects. Here, we made new friends, had new adventures, and learned new things. Building connections with people that would forever hold a special place in our hearts, learning new hobbies that would become part of our life's joys, and preparing us for what would be a new beginning. We were open. Never to fail, always to grow.

See, by now it was ingrained in me. Upward movement only. Never going backward. Living in the projects, I was drawn to things that filled me with joy. It was here that I befriended our elderly neighbor. My first friend in our new home. I was fascinated by the way she created the art she so effortlessly crafted with her hands. I'd neither seen nor heard of it. The way she weaved the yarn through the plastic squares was intriguing. 'What was she making?' I thought. So, I sat with her. On the steps of our conjoined home, outside in our breezeway, we had many talks. I watched as she created piece after piece of her plastic canvas stitching, never knowing what she was creating until she was done, and she never gave it away to keep me guessing. What I loved most was watching it transform from nothing into something. The valuable lessons I learned that would carry on with me through life.

But this wasn't my only pastime in our new environment. Sitting on these steps across from a basketball court, the center of the projects, I watched as the boys played ball. This was my opportunity to be a kid again. I just wanted to forget all the chaos that had consumed my life before this move. I loved basketball. Once again, the tomboy in me. I wanted to challenge myself. Push past my introverted ways and let my skills speak for themselves. One year, I asked for only one thing for Christmas…a basketball. Elated to receive the gift I vowed to take on the court, I'd peer outside our kitchen window with views of the desolate court some days and took advantage of its vacancy to practice my moves. Weaving the basketball in between my legs like a pro. Circling the three-point line and mastering my free throws for the opportunity to play ball with the boys and show them I was a force to be reckoned with. Extending myself by impressing the guys with my shots from the mid-court line ultimately granted me permission to play along. And I held my own. I moved on to trying out for my school's team and getting involved in more extracurricular activities during this time. Could it be that I was finally starting to feel like a normal kid again?

Living in the projects, I was also drawn to the Sunday morning calls of the children's Bible Study group. Every Sunday, at the same time . . . must have been 8 or 9 a.m., when I could hear the call of the Bible group leader say, "Yogi Bear . . . Sun-day-school!!!" followed by the repetition of the kids behind him. Intrigued, I'd rush to the window to see what the hype was about. I'd see the kids run out of the buildings and file in line, reminiscent of the Pied Piper, only a more positive version of said scary tale. I knew better than to ask my mother to be a part of this group. My mother was very protective of us at this time. It could have been all the things she had recently experienced with my brother that catapulted her into an extreme need to watch over us. And as she expressed time and time again, she didn't know these people. Who knew where they were taking us? Though it was clear that these kids "survived" the Bible study group, it was merely a scene for me to watch each day. It brought me joy to hear each morning, "Yogi, beeeaarrrrr . . . Sun-day-schoooool!" To this day, I can recite those words just as symphonically as I'd heard them the first time.

The spiritual bug had been ingrained in me by now. Not that we attended church on a regular basis, but because my mother always took advantage of opportunities to expose us to religion. We've been in Kingdom Halls as Jehovah's Witnesses and attended the Church of Seventh Day Adventist,

Baptist Church, Catholic Church, and Pentecostal Church. You name it, we've been there. I'm grateful it provided us with the ability to see and experience the many ways people worship. It allowed us to make a more sound decision regarding our beliefs, holding no judgment toward the practices individually, more so, understanding how similar the practice of Christianity was in all. For me, it felt like a saving grace. Literally. The connection I had to being in the house of the Lord, no matter which house it was, made me feel safe, secure, loved, and cared for. I was determined to seek this kind of love for the rest of my days.

Not having any connection to music in particular, I couldn't distinguish between what's considered secular music versus gospel music. To me, it was simply music. A vibe. A feeling. I felt it in ways I also felt the Word of God when I read it, that is, as much as my twelve-year-old mind could decipher. It was the early '90s. The days of "The Jukebox" where we could call the hotline and request our favorite music videos to be played. My favorite artist at the time was Mary J. Blige. There was something so real about her. Her dance moves spoke to the creative side of me. The music group "Jade" did the same thing. It opened me up to the idea of love. Not just romantic love but love in general. I saw it play out with my older sister, as she had a crush back then. I began to see that I was growing up and understanding more. Yet, still engrossed in my own little world, remaining school-focused and art-focused and trying to break out of my box. The box I had created for myself because of past hurt and traumas.

And so we lived life, just the four of us. My mother, my two sisters, and me in our own little bubble. Making the best of our circumstances. By this time, my father had moved out of state for work. He had traveled away so many times we didn't even think anything of it. It wasn't odd not to have him around. We still spoke to him, and he checked on us often, but physically his presence wasn't there. It became the norm. Our norm.

I think back to these times, and I realize how little we knew about my mother's adult life. She was always so careful to shield us from things we didn't need to know. Her focus, first and foremost, was to raise three strong women. She did that in many ways by ensuring that we were on top of our chores and our studies. Though I will say, it was miraculous to me just how well we were able to hold ourselves account-able for our schoolwork and responsibilities, knowing that my mother neither read nor spoke any English. She didn't check our homework; she didn't understand how to read report cards, and she didn't concern herself so much with our school life because it was almost as if we knew we had to take a handle on it all on our own. She made it clear that we were to get good grades, respect our teachers, and do our work but never micro-managed us. Well, not for me at least. My older sister marched to the tune of her own drum. Yet, she could still maintain a *C* average. She was the kid who always got the "she talks too much in class" notes. And I was quite the opposite.

Chapter 5
FAMILY TIES

I t was summertime in the early '90s, and Hurricane Andrew was inching its way toward Florida. My mother sent us to Miami to visit my aunt, uncle, and cousins. I imagine she used this time to get her affairs in order. Dealing with my brother's deportation, she had a lot to consider. Though we were living our best summer lives in Florida, not once did we ever consider what she was up to. After all, everything was "fine." My aunt and uncle made it a point to entertain us in so many ways on our trip to Florida. We visited the beach, we joined them on their "gambling dates" as I called them. We enjoyed playing in the arcade while they bet on Jai Alai, on the Greyhounds, or played Bingo. It was all new to us, but we were obedient. I actually believe I enjoyed it much more than my sister, as I recall there were many times I'd willingly joined them on my own. She, happy to stay behind with my cousins at home as they hung out with their friends. And there were also times we tagged along with their friends at my aunt and uncle's orders. Never feeling like the pesky little cousins, they made us feel quite included.

This made for memories we would cherish forever—like the time one of my cousins gave in to my annoying request to drive her bright yellow Chevy Chevette into the driveway and nearly knocked down the house when I confused the brake pedal for the gas. Oops! My aunt was inside preparing dinner. She was a little shaken up, but it was merely brushed off with a shake of the head and a few choice words. Good times! Our summer escapades would soon come to an end.

We managed to return home right in the nick of time. Hurricane Andrew turned into a Category 5 storm that would devastate the Bahamas, Florida, and Louisiana, causing over $27 billion in damages in late August 1992. My mother was a nervous wreck. I recall sitting by her side as she made attempt after attempt to contact her brother and her sister-in-law. Checking on my cousins and the family became a daily affair at that moment. The devastation seen on the news was earth-shattering. There were mass casualties and losses of homes all along the coast and inland. We'd later find that our family's home, thankfully, was fine. But it was hard to reach them for days due to down power lines. No electricity or phone lines meant we had to find creative ways to reach one another. My uncle found a pay phone my mother could dial at a certain time to reach him when the home phone lines were down. My mother did what she knew best and began collecting items to send for relief. Her ability to kick into high gear at the most difficult times has always been her strong suit. Failure was not an option. It was always, by any means necessary.

It wasn't long after this that my mother decided it was time to leave Rhode Island behind. Though the news was a surprise, I was ready for the change. We had gotten a taste of Miami, and I felt quite fond of the place. Knowing we'd be close to our cousins was a treat for me, considering we had connected in a special way during the summer. Tagging along with their high school friends and spending time with my aunt and uncle reminded me just how much we needed to be closer to family. I imagine this was my mother's sentiment as well—that it was time to start anew. We would always ask my mother when our father was coming home. She'd just say, "Soon." He'd echo the same. Year after year went by and he didn't show. I saw my mother's light dim even more so from this point forward. Still, maintaining a firm stand and ensuring we were on track but imagine a mother with two teenage girls and a child. The lack of a father figure was truly missed in our home. Maybe I'm speaking for myself here, but I saw how that lack of protection was affecting us.

The change of scenery was good for us, though. We settled into a home my uncle and aunt found for us. It just so happened that it used to be the home of my aunt's sister. She had moved just up the block and they deemed this was the perfect opportunity for us to live close by. This home reminded me of our home in Puerto Rico. I recall the back room of the home, the sunroom, having the very cement-style floors our sunroom in Puerto Rico had. Painted red and speckled with sparkling tiles. I was feeling at home already. It was surrounded by glass paneled windows which were reminiscent of the old windows that existed back in the 1940s. The ones you'd have to wind open and close. It was a spacious three-bedroom home. One of the bedrooms was soon to be the one my sisters and I would argue over, as it seemed to have the most privacy and its own door leading outside. Something to work toward, we thought sneakily. My aunt and uncle lived only a few blocks away, so it would be rather convenient for us all as we learned to navigate the neighborhood and this new adventure. My mother signed us up for school. Both my older sister and I attended middle school together initially until my sister transitioned to high school, leaving me behind. My little sister continued her elementary school education. We'd meet new friends, get acclimated, and start fresh once again.

During this time in our lives, rebelling in our teens was inevitable. We started to push the envelope more and more. My sister and I spent nights out past curfew, knowing there were serious repercussions waiting for us at home. We tested the waters more and more. What happened to me? Though school was still at the forefront of my responsibilities, and my grades continued to reflect it, my behavior at home became less and less cooperative. These were the times when I wish we had our father around. We certainly didn't want to cause our mother any hurt, but it's like we just couldn't control it. Hormonal shifts in "teenagerhood" is a real thing. Though, at the time, I didn't understand nor acknowledge it, looking back at it now and seeing the very rebellious behaviors of my child, it became painfully clear.

I met my "first love" at this time. At fourteen, I was over the moon with a boy four years my elder. I was still in middle school, and he was in high school. He lived across the street from us. I can't recall exactly how the love connection occurred, but I did spend a lot of time outside hanging out with neighboring kids. We innocently listened to music, danced, and played video games. While my mother was at work, I'd spend time with my boyfriend on his porch, which led to spending time in his living room. That led to, well, I think you know where I'm going with this. I lost my virginity at the tender age of fourteen. Just thinking about that now makes me sick to my stomach. In fact, it pains me, saddens me, and reminds me of what a dark time this was. Though in the moment I felt like I was living it up and getting away with it, deep inside I felt broken. Losing myself more and more each day. It was at this moment that I experienced some more trauma. From being a victim of a robbery while I waited outside my middle school classroom portable to becoming a victim of dating violence.

Yes, dating violence. Much like domestic violence, dating violence occurs in dating relationships between teenagers and can follow one into adulthood. What I had experienced in my childhood had been a different form of violation. Intentional physical contact made to hurt me was nothing I'd dealt with outside of sibling rivalry. My older sister and I had more than one physical run-in as we had differences of opinions growing up. Going to blows when neither one of us would get our way became our new form of communication. But this? This felt different.

Being slapped across the face by my then-boyfriend because he was angry that I was talking to another guy while we were broken up was a new level of low. I felt demeaned, ridiculed, and embarrassed as this occurred right outside my home. As I stood on the opposite side of the fence from him, he reached across and smacked me so hard, my mother's family friend (who we so lovingly called our grandmother) came out running to see what the commotion was about. Easily distinguishing the sound of a smack, she was ready to kick his butt though he very quickly walked away as he saw her approach. I later considered this a "love tap." Looking at that incident as a statement of his "love" for me. Having accepted his apology, we continued dating. And I begged my grandmother not to speak a word of it to my mother upon her return. I imagine my mother was out of state during this time either visiting my father or in the Dominican Republic handling some kind of family emergency. This kind of reaction wasn't uncommon you see? Quite a sensible response to what a young girl who hadn't experienced a sense of love and protection in her home would feel.

There was a long talk had with my adoptive grandma thereafter. She encouraged me. In her own Panamanian words, she lifted me up. Looking to comfort me yes, but more importantly she was feeding me a sense of worth, value, and standard. A conversation, although lodged deep in the back of my mind thereafter, I would never forget. These words of encouragement would serve me in the future, though at that very moment, I didn't see it. I didn't relate to the young girl she was describing as she saw me. Somehow, somewhere, I lost my sense of self.

In search of self, I recalled the words of my favorite grade school teacher as we carried out the last days of school before moving from Providence. Connecting myself with a time that brought me joy really did help me stay connected to the part of myself that wanted more out of life. Mrs. Mullins was the English teacher I would never forget. She believed in me in such a manner I'd never had anyone believe in me before. She saw talent in my writing that made me realize I did, in fact, have a gift. She exposed me to literary legends that would forever hold a special place in my heart. Writers like Shakespeare, Dickens, Hemingway, Poe, Mark Twain, Wilde, Emily Dickinson, Maya Angelou, and more. They were my inspiration. They helped me escape from the reality of life in a way that I needed more than ever in those times. Mrs. Mullins would forever be unforgettable to me. She introduced me not only to writing but also created in me a love for reading. For escaping into a world full of joy and wonder.

I was saddened yet fascinated by the way Mrs. Mullins could carry on despite her disability. It was clearly visible. She looked frail. A slim yet tall and full of life mature woman, she was. Her lips were as thin and dry as paper. Her fingers . . . deformed and bent out of shape as if she suffered from arthritis. Still, this didn't stop her from pointing at things, at us, or using her hands ever so carefully to write on the chalkboard. Her eyes seen small through the thick eyeglass she donned, brown, and sunken into her face as if protecting themselves from the elements. Her hair was always well groomed, each curl carefully placed around her face. Mrs. Mullins suffered from a disease called Anhidrosis.[7] She explained it was her inability to sweat due to sweat glands that didn't function as they should, to remove heat and cool down the body. For this reason, she shared that she always traveled in the summer to cold climates.

It saddened me to think that such a lovely person could experience such hardship. We built a special connection, so much so, that when I informed her we were moving out of state, she encouraged me to keep writing by sending her pen pal letters. So I did. Somewhere along the years, I stopped receiving return letters from her. I made various attempts to reach her, penning letters even addressed to her family looking for answers on her whereabouts, fearing the worst had happened and she may have succumbed to her disease. I never heard from her again. But she was a source of light for me. Hearing her words of encouragement in my head as if I was still at Carl G. Lauro Elementary School.

This helped bring me back down to earth, reminding me of where I came from and the tender and genuine moments of my life. And so life went on. The days turned into nights, and I worked diligently to keep my head in the books. Before long, it was time for my middle school graduation, yes . . . all this occurred before I even entered high school. In my mother's attempt to uproot us from the neighborhood she so seemingly despised, she decided it was time for a change. Yes, again. Maybe she was beginning to feel like she need to reel us in a bit. A change of environment would do us good. She heard amazing things about a new high school opening at the start of my freshman year. Before you knew it, we were registered and ready to move along. Moving my sister from then Miami

Jackson Senior High School, which was becoming more vola-tile by the day. The school was located in the same Allapattah neighborhood where I was robbed of my treasured 24-carat gold nameplate chain. Hialeah Gardens became our new home, but only for a few weeks into the school year because, as you would guess . . . yes, it was time to move, yet again. We weren't prepared for the turn of events that followed. I only imagine that conversations between my parents led to the need to be together again. I couldn't be mad at that. We'd done enough damage these last few years—certainly had put her nerves on edge. Leaving my then "boyfriend" behind didn't affect me one way or another; deep inside, I knew he was no good for me.

Chapter 6

LEAN ON ME

So back up north we went. To the bustling town of Paterson, New Jersey. This time…back with my father. I was ecstatic to finally be back in his arms. His loving embrace and bold demeanor were something we longed for. He was rough on the outside, but we knew he had a sweet spot for us. He was mush inside, as he'd let us get away with things we shouldn't have. While it was a joyous occasion, it was clear that this move was very sudden. Not only was it unlike my mother to pick up and go without having a plan in place, but for her to not even have a stable place to live? This was *new*. Surely there had to have been a reason. It felt a little rushed to me, a quite unfamiliar space. But we did what we did best, we rolled with it. My father was living with his nephew. The nephew he had moved in with to help build his business, or at least this is what we were told. We slept on the floor during this transition, but it truly didn't even matter because we were finally all together. I'm sure this was hard on my mother, though. This was not what she was accustomed to. She'd always provided us with a roof over our heads and a dedicated space. This . . . this was different.

So the task of finding a new school was priority number one. Although we were zoned for the infamous Eastside High School, my older sister and I were shaking in our boots at the mere thought of having to attend a school known for its violence. Word on the street was that not much had changed since the days of Mr. Clark as is depicted in the movie *Lean on Me*. So, we were on a mission to convince our parents to enroll us in private school. After all, our cousin attended one, why couldn't we? This is when we realized that private school costs money. Lots of it! And though, in our minds, money was no object for our safety; our parents, who'd be paying for it, had another view. They just simply could not afford it. So with tear-filled eyes, and after many heated discussions about our concern for our safety, they still sent us away to "fair Eastside." But I had a plan.

I had convinced our father that I needed a phone to use in case of an emergency. I also felt I needed to make myself as invisible as possible. You know, to blend with the crowd. My father gave me his only spare cell phone. A then "brick phone" as they called them. Also known as the Motorola DynaTac 8000x. Ideal, as I imagined if I had to use it to throw across someone's head in self-defense, I would! Truly an embarrassment to be seen with, especially since cellphones had advanced to flip phones, but I couldn't care less. I placed my brick phone in my backpack, activated and ready to use in case of an emergency. I specially requested baggy pants and T-shirts and a large jacket with timberland boots as my first day of school outfit. I needed to fit in. I needed to camouflage. And so I did.

My sister, on the other hand, couldn't help herself. Always the social butterfly, she showed up with baggy pants, stylish shoes, a form-fitting top, and red lipstick that popped. Sure to be noticed. I didn't want to be seen anywhere near her. She'd make me a target, and I just wanted to fade into the background. It wasn't long before she had gained a group of friends. These friends were surprised beyond belief to hear that I was her sister. I was that smart quiet girl in their classes. Though they were all a year ahead of me, my studious attitude had caught up with me. I was now in the space of a more mature crowd. A humble and well-established crowd. I began to loosen up. Entering my sophomore year, I was more at ease. Even though I witnessed some horrific things during my freshman year, I would soon be reading about those very experiences, and worse, when I was assigned as editor of the school newspaper. A position I know would have made Mrs. Mullins proud.

The graphic accounts of student experiences were not that far-fetched from what was depicted in the movie. Students witnessing the most horrific aggressive interactions between others. Bullying to the extreme. None were concerned with the potential of expulsion or school suspension. In these moments, it was a survival of the fittest. Every man for themselves. Some of them expressed just how gravely these experiences affected them. And they weren't too far off from what I had experienced as well. I recall, during my freshman year, walking out of the lunchroom after a very isolated lunch (the norm for me),

I heard the hustle and bustle of commotion ahead of me. As I walked down the narrow corridor leading to the open hallway of the first floor in the west wing of the school, I reached the end of this "tunnel," and I saw it. A long smear of blood along the wall. The altercation was already over by the time I witnessed the aftermath. The victim and responsible party, long gone. But it left me wondering. Lord, how will they ever get through the school year after this? I didn't even know them, but I was anxious for them.

This moment, like many others during my tenure at Eastside High School, left me speechless. Only processing as much as my thoughts would allow, given I had no other choice but to show up each day praying that I wouldn't be a target. And just as is usually the case in these teenage years, soon that was all a memory. I built friendships within my circle that were bonds I'd cherish for the rest of my days. After all, we were showing up, hoping for the same during these times. Counting down the days to graduation. Or, simply creating "skip breaks" for ourselves that would help us pass the time.

It was in these "skip breaks" that I'd realize just how nonchalant my mother would be and how quickly she was to trust our judgment. In hindsight, seeing all she was going through at the time, I can only assume she just wanted to believe. To believe that we were honest, open, and true. In a way, this made us want to be just that all the more. We didn't want to let her down. I'll never forget the day my mother saw my best friend and I walking down the street just south of the school. We made our way through the chain-locked side doors of the school that day and headed toward downtown Paterson. Our goal? To go shopping. I don't even recall having money to buy much. My job at my uncle's supermarket was paying me some cash; however, I don't believe it was enough to go on a shopping spree on Main St. Yet, it was definitely an escape. And I believe my mother knew this. Granting us a ride downtown and dropping us off. I was shocked and impressed all at once.

Some days, our group would crash at each other's homes. Skipping school for us certainly came second to our school responsibilities. I recall us arranging our time of departure based on the completion of our school assignments or term examinations. Only then could we fully enjoy ourselves. I bet you're wondering what we did on these skip days. Most teenagers would have taken this opportunity to do all our parents told us not to do. Drink, smoke, etc. But nope! Not us. For us, it was a chance to truly enjoy each other's company. We laughed, we joked, we cooked, we ate, and we listened to music. And we did it all again at the next opportunity. We looked forward to these moments of relief. So wrapped up in our own little bubble of socialization that we didn't consider what our parents were doing, how they were feeling, or what they were going through. We just knew "it was none of our business," as we were raised and most accustomed to believing. They were adults. Whatever they were going through, surely they could handle.

During our time living in Paterson, my mother received the dreaded call informing her of our grandmother's passing. Our grandfather had passed away some years earlier, but my grandmother's passing would be a surefire contention in our family. Little did we know just how much my mother's familial relationships had been negatively affected over the years. Sibling rivalries were sparked in that period of time. For reasons unknown to us, we just saw the family continue to drift apart. Our financial restrictions wouldn't allow us to be present for our grandmother's funeral. As kids, all we could do was grieve from afar. It was during the initial years of high school we had gotten the chance to spend more time with our grandmother. Yes, we had done so earlier in our childhood, but it surely was different traveling to the Dominican Republic in our teen years. Our focus was different, but so was our appreciation for all that surrounded us.

Those of us who grew up in the Dominican Republic in these times or visited family can recall the infamous "*se fue la luz!*" moments. Translation, "the power went out!" For most living in civilization, this was a tragic moment. A moment of panic and unrest. For us, it was nostalgic. Exciting to say the least. This meant most people would be forced to light their gas lamps in order to see and get around the house. Most chores took a back seat during this time as well. Some people laid down to sleep, while others were led to the "*marquesina,*" also known as the front porch to rock in the rocking chairs, listen to music, play dominoes, and simply enjoy the moment. This was the reason for the excitement of these moments. To this day, these *se fue la luz!* moments still occur. Unless you are fortunate enough to have a backup generator, of course— though most living in the city weren't as privileged. My grandmother certainly wasn't, but it was never even necessary. Staying there, we felt as though we were privileged. She lacked nothing.

I say all this to say . . . so much was going on in our family at the time; and, though we were well aware of it, not once did we ever feel like we were in jeopardy. On the contrary, we felt safe. We felt protected. We felt heard, things you want to feel in your home life. See, my mom did an outstanding job of rolling with the punches. Even after years of living in New Jersey, she was always focused on upward movement. Hoping to start a new life, a much-needed transition was soon to come.

My older sister graduated from Eastside High School in 1998. And she did it with a bun in the oven. Yes, my sister was one of the many kids who are part of the statistic not many want to speak of—the teenage parent statistic. Our parents didn't believe in any other way to deal with this than to, you guessed it, keep on trucking. I believe my mother was also at a crossroads with our father at that moment. Maybe she also looked at this as a welcomed blessing. I sensed some tension between our parents due to my father's tendency to put other things before her "needs." The consideration of uprooting our family was an ultimatum of sorts. I recall having been on the other side of the wall while they had this discussion, which they were so careful to keep quiet. Needless to say, my mother had decided. If there was something she was good at, it was being decisive. She found it was a better time than any to move back to Florida.

Chapter 7

BACK TO BASICS

My mother had already gone ahead a few months before to scope out the area with a long-time friend to whom she'd leave the responsibility of finding a good home for her. This longtime friend, by the way, happened to be the mother of my very first boyfriend. Yes, truly a full-circle moment here. Our family grew close over the years. We'd seen each other through much in these times. So it was no surprise that their bond was such that she could trust her with this endeavor. Once it was confirmed that we found what would be my mother's first home purchase here in the "States," it wasn't long before we were beginning to pack up for the major move. True to form, things wouldn't go as smoothly as she'd hoped.

We were aware that things wouldn't be easy. However, having moved many times before in our childhood, and with no real solidified anchor to those places, we were open to it. This time, even more so as it was not an unfamiliar place. In fact, it felt like home. The same place we lived just years before moving to New Jersey, as a matter of fact. We had established a familiarity with the environment and, even beyond that, we knew this was a matriarchal foundation. Almost instantly, upon arriving in Miami, there was a sense of belonging. A sense of peace. For my older sister, however, there was unease not knowing what she would embark on as a parent but open to the possibilities. For my little sister, a sense of insecurity yet a great sense of adventure. She would grow into her own in the years to follow. For me, a major sense of responsibility. Somehow, as the only person in the household with employment (employed at Lady Foot Locker in the hustle and bustle of Downtown Miami), I was just like my mother, ready to take on the task.

And so it became that they depended on me. Or so I imagined. At least, this is how I carried on. Graciously providing as best as I could with what I earned at the time. These summer months, I worked feverishly to ensure I provided a hefty contribution to the household. My work involved the ability to make a commission on sales and, having been placed at one of the hotspots of tourist destinations near the port of Miami, I was eager to prove just how great of a worker I was. Though my father sent money to help pay the bills, those funds would soon become scarcer and scarcer. Until, in fact, they were non-existent. Or from what we could tell anyhow. Our daily food intake consisted of white rice and chicken. It was fulfilling and inexpensive for a family of four. We loved it. The splurging was left to my older sister and her cravings and for my little sister who was, how I shall say it . . . SPOILED.

Sure enough, my mother did what we know her to do; she refocused, got a new game plan, and found employment. In my eyes, the first "real" official job I think she's ever had since we moved from the Dominican Republic, outside of her own stylistic entrepreneurial ventures. I recall seeing her wearing her uniform to work each day and I was proud, like a mother seeing her child off on the first day of school. We supported her. And just like that, we became, yet again, our usual girl bunch. It was a home full of estrogen. And with the new baby on the way, things would get all the more exciting.

It should be noted that we were now also moving back near my family, the cousins with whom we had grown up. My mother's brother soon also became a staple male figure in our household. One of the youngest of their sibling group, my uncle looked up to my mother. Shortly to follow, another uncle joined us in Miami, bringing his wife and daughter from the Dominican Republic for a better life (as is often believed by many foreigners. After all, we were considered the Free World with loads of potential right?). Soon after, more of our family from Providence, Rhode Island came down to Miami as well. We welcomed my mother's youngest sister, my cousin, and her two young boys. What started as a lonesome matriarchal expedition among us four had now grown into a loving group.

As a family, we hustled. With one thing in mind, *success*. We'd see it no other way. We were on a mad dash toward financial freedom and not taking no for an answer. Great examples surrounded us. The start of my senior year in high school would also prove to be the most nonchalant year of my life. I knew I was ahead of the game and was excited to hear I qualified to be in the OJT Program, where on-the-job training allowed me to leave early each day to get to work. As studious as ever, once again, my goal became to keep my head down, get to class, do my work, and leave. This time, my eyes were laser-focused on my goals: to continue to contribute toward my household and learn the skills needed to reach new heights in sales. Friendships weren't at the forefront of my mind. After all, I had friends already. All-be-it thousands of miles away in New Jersey, but I had them. We vowed to always stay in touch. A bond so strong we believed it was unbreakable. No other friendships would compare, and so yes, I was shocked when one particular classmate was adamant about me staying a few minutes behind during lunch to hang out with her friend group. Did you hear what I said? I was focused.

Uninterested. Making up an excuse each and every time and glad that those excuses were actually true. I had to go to work. But one day, in her persistent demeanor, she asked again, and this time she was not taking no for an answer. I didn't have to work this particular afternoon, so I was able to hang out for a little while. This group soon became my new-found friend group, of which only a few select people would really draw my attention. But that one persistent Dominican firecracker friend of mine would hold a place in my heart forever. We've told the story so often over the years and we laugh each and every time. Especially when we recall the times she chose to sleep through class and then turn to me just moments before class was over, asking that I catch her up. I'll admit, oftentimes, I even gave her the answers. To be young again!

My Lady Foot Locker job was starting to offer more opportunities for leadership roles. Now having transferred to a mall location near my home, I had gained the trust of my current manager who vouched for my position as shift manager. This meant longer nights, closing shifts, and responsibility for reports and bank deposits at the end of the day. I was ecstatic. At last, my hard work was paying off. I was even called upon to close a different location. One I was unfamiliar with, but the job would be all the same. So I took it on like a champ, walking in there like I'd been doing this for years. They knew I had been well-recommended, and I made them proud each time.

I'll never forget getting paid and bringing the money home to my mother, only asking for a minimal amount for gas and snacks. Knowing that the bulk of the funds were needed to pay the bills, it was okay with me. But now I had been working many long shifts. Long shifts turned into long days where standing, climbing ladders in the stockroom, and walking was 98 percent of my job's function. My knees were aching, as were my feet. I knew it was time for a new pair of shoes—a more supportive and comfortable pair that would help ease the discomfort at work. So, hesitantly, I asked, "Is it okay if I keep a few extra dollars to buy myself a pair of shoes?" My mother was truly flabbergasted by the request. She said, "Well, of course! You didn't even need to ask me. You work hard and you deserve it." She went on to thank me for helping as I had been. I realized at that moment, it was the first time I'd heard her say it. Not that I was in any way expecting it; after all, it was the least I could do after all she's done for us.

I know by now you're wondering, well, what about your older sister? Did she work? Did she contribute? My sister was getting further along in her pregnancy. At this point, she was reaching nine months' gestation and about ready to pop. Our bundle of joy (my niece) was born into this world in September 1998. Only about a month or so into my senior year in high school. I was eager to get home to help as much as I could with her care. My sister was grateful for the break we provided as we were clearly all over her. I believe that, because my sister had her so young, she wanted to make up for lost time. Though she was an amazing mother, and cared well for her daughter, she also struggled with the need to be herself in a world she had still so much to experience. Totally natural. Being the fun-loving personality she was, she would soon find new outlets to explore her youth. My best friend also became close friends with her as would her sister. And so began the nights out on the town.

While I ensured to maintain a "balance" with school, work, and play . . . my sister's life would become more play. But she was always this way. Fun-loving and full of life. She made sure to live each moment to the fullest nonetheless, vowing to push through two years of school to obtain her Business Administration degree. Something my mother was very proud of, an accomplishment she would forever hold for the rest of her life. No one could ever take that away from her. She contributed once she could go back to work after the baby. But in true older sister fashion, her priorities were always her first, and the rest would follow. A quality I quite admired as I grew into adulthood, I must say. In the moment, however, I'll admit I was a bit spiteful. But we've always been different in that way. My life's goal was and always has been to make my mother proud. Even at the expense of my happiness. I'd quickly learn how this would backfire on me in the years to follow. So, yes, if I could turn the hands of time, I'd sit and say to my sister, "Show me your ways!"

Chapter 8

LIFE GOES ON

My mother continued to work on ways to maximize her investment. My uncle, a general contractor and construction extraordinaire, soon came up with the genius idea to create an efficiency from the part of the home that was a second living room option. It would help toward payment of the mortgage and provide her with the ease and flexibility she needed to cover all the household expenses. This efficiency became one, then two, then three, then . . . well, let's just say she didn't have to worry about how the mortgage was getting paid. In fact, she now became a full-fledged landlord with other worries and responsibilities, most of which she took head-on. She was strong, opinionated, no nonsense, and she held her own. Here we are over twenty years later, and those efficiencies still hold strong.

Of course, she didn't give up on her natural skill in cosmetology. She always made sure to create a space in the home for her hair salon. This space was a convenient place for us all when it was time to get pampered. Something we'd grown quite accustomed to over the years, given that we've been sitting in a salon since conception. This, yet another staple in our lives. The salon represented to my mother, and would soon represent to us, the very thing that catapulted her dreams, her successes, her resilience, and perseverance. For us, it was always a nostalgic thing to come home to. A room full of women chit-chatting about family matters and life goals, sharing recipes and sometimes secrets. It was an outlet for many. Soon word got out to friends and family that she was able to pamper them too. And so she once again began what would now be considered as a side hustle. Coincidentally, it was a welcome transition, given that she had been laid off from her job. We weren't panicked about this, as our financial stability was certainly looking up— to where I could keep most of my money now. Imagine that! Splurging on newly released discounted sneakers from work and arguing with my little sister for borrowing them without permission. She was a sneaky one. A new life had now begun. A freer life, with more liberties. Then came more adventures.

At this point you may also be wondering what ever happened to my father. As I sit here typing this, I'm trying to recall if we were ever in contact during this time. I believe we did. Though it wasn't often, I recall many times my mother would be on the phone with him and hand over the phone for us to say hello. The conversations were short and sweet. He'd ask how we were doing, how the new baby was coming along, how school was and how we were getting acclimated. It was always pleasant talking to our father. He reminded me of a time where

I felt loved and secure. He provided that for us as children even though he and my mother's relationship had their own set of difficulties. As children, we were never privy to those struggles. I'm grateful for that because it allowed me to build a bond that was one of a kind, loving, and safe.

After graduating high school, I immediately enrolled in college. My initial intent was to select a career in which schooling was quick to complete and allow me to gain employment that would benefit my family. I started looking at the field of hospitality. After all, the city of Miami was one big touristic destination. Why not capitalize on this and establish a career that would ensure provision for my family for years to come? Not that I was assigned this responsibility, but in my mind, it just made sense. I didn't want to see my mother struggle any more than we had previously. Now that I could do something about it, why not? Totally and completely disregarding any of my own personal wants. But, at that time, I was okay with that. The scholarship I received to attend this university was an added bonus. All the more reason to get started right away. Until, that is, I walked into the school with my mother for a tour and orientation.

The advisor went on to tell me all about their degree programs and, when she got to the Criminal Justice degree, I was intrigued. But I continued to point her in the direction of hospitality. She asked me the one question that would quickly change my mind. "Why hospitality?" At that moment, as I phrased my response as eloquently as I could, I realized that was a less than impressive reason to decide on a career opportunity. I wasn't in any way passionate about the field. My only motivation for it was the earning potential and how quickly I'd be done with the program. Saying it out loud, I realized just how silly of a reason that was to choose a career. Time and money were going to be invested in something I would later regret. When my mother heard my reasoning, she, too, was flabbergasted. Like, *what?!* She quickly encouraged me to study something I was passionate about.

Jokingly over the years, my mother would always refer to me as the "*policia.*" A policewoman. A woman of the law. Be it because I was always a serious child, very democratic at best, poised and no nonsense with a strong-willed temperament. These wonderful characteristics, the advisor described as best for their Criminal Justice program. Seems I'd fit right in. As she explained it further, I was sold. The life goals scribbled in my middle school memory book would soon come true. I've always had a heart for public service. In fact, I've always had a heart to serve, PERIOD. There was something about me that always strived to help others, as evidenced by everything you've read so far. I was selfless in many ways, looking to put a smile on others' faces, but mostly my mother. Hurt people would always find me and I would always serve them. Willingly, lovingly, selflessly. That was it, I decided to enroll in the Bachelor of Arts in Criminal Justice Program. This was the start of many changes in my daily life.

Now, I was a college student, so I needed a "real" job, I thought. One that would work with my school schedule. Back in the late 90s, there was a call center in Miami Gardens called Precision Response Corporation. For some reason—likely the fact that the main hiring requirement was a high school diploma—many high school graduates worked here. And it helped that my older sister was already there. She put in a good word for me. I applied and guess what? I got the job. My work schedule was Monday through Friday, 9 a.m. to 5 p.m. 'My first real nine to five,' I thought as I gazed into the distance. (Cue the dramatics.) The American dream (sarcastically speaking, of course)! It was time to move on past my retail position at Lady Foot Locker. A bittersweet moment, seeing as how it was pivotal to the development of what I now consider the best work ethic. It truly helped me establish my professional identity. For that, I will always be grateful, but it was time. Time to grow. Time to challenge myself. Time to fly. It would only be the beginning. And so I went on my fearless pursuit of growth into young adulthood.

As I carried on during this time, I would soon meet a man that changed the trajectory of my life forever. I, the young call taker on the other end of the line, answering calls for DirecTV, and he was my shift supervisor. He carried himself with professional poise and had a special swag about him. His speech, his mannerisms, his attention ultimately won me over. And though I could kind of tell he was a bit of a lady's man (red flag), I was still open to giving him a chance. He began to pursue me at work, a welcomed act as far as I was concerned. No "Me Too" movement aggressors here. Only one thing caused my hesitation: he really wasn't "my type." I usually gravitated toward the same personality with a more ethnic vibe. A gentleman of more caramel complexion but he was nice. That was the first and last time I'd challenge myself to "think outside the box" in the dating pool. I mean, let's be honest. We all know ourselves, right? We know what we're attracted to and can quickly pin-point the things that we aren't attracted to. Shortly, our conversations gravitated from within the confines of the PRC building to talking on a more frequent basis outside of work. Spending one-on-one time together helped me see more of his real personality. And though there were more red flags (he smoked, and I'm not talking Newports here), I was willing to work with it. Why? I don't know. I was young, vulnerable, naïve, and smitten. All the things that would cause us to become less able to make a sound judgment call on the matters of the heart.

Our "relationship" grew to one of a more romantic nature, making it a bit awkward in the workplace. Pretending that we weren't seeing each other, we'd carry on as if we weren't just on the phone for hours the night before, chatting away. And as things progressed in our relationship, we were thankful for the opportunity to find a more lucrative employment opportunity. He was granted a pretty legit position with a telecommunications company. Another call center of sorts but this time dealing mainly with the customer service aspect of this agency which provided telecommunication services to residents. Again, being the boss, he was now able to offer me a position with more responsibility and higher pay. I welcomed the change, seeing as how things were starting to get a little weird at DirecTV and, frankly, the scripted customer service position was just dreadfully painful to get through. I mean, how natural can a conversation be when you have to literally read the prompts off the screen? Most days, I felt like a robot. I was elated to have been offered this new opportunity and felt it couldn't have come at a better time. Until I regretted it, that is.

This telecommunications agency was privately owned by some investors from Nigeria. There were rumors that they were starting to struggle financially to keep the business afloat. I was ever so vigilant of all the administrators' moves, hoping to get enough information to cut loose in a reasonable amount of time before things went south. As things started to fall apart within the organization, so it was in our relationship as well. It seems my boyfriend's position of power and authority was starting to get to his head. At this point, blatantly flirting with other women right in front of me. The women knew we were involved, yet also entertained him. The icing on the cake came the day I was confronted by his girlfriend. Yes! You read that right. According to him, they were broken up, but this woman had a different story to tell.

Oh, just the typical post-high school grad drama right? While I was experiencing the inevitable woes of life, my mother continued to progress with her home-based business and landlord duties. Always looking to make new improvements to the home, her over-zealous and ambitious goals for the property were starting to catch up with her. Credit cards maxed out and payments close to late. Sometimes, even missing a few, coming really close to losing what she had worked so hard to attain. But with every problem comes a solution. We were able to get the property sold. Who was the new property owner, you ask? Well, *me*, of course. Anything to save our home. Though I'm sure the mortgage provider may have looked at the loan request and did a double take. There was nothing holding me back from purchasing a home in my now twenty years of age. Yup. And so it was. My first home ownership experience was one that would be short-lived, granting my mother enough time to bring herself out of the financial mess she created. I then sold the property right back. It was the only option we had to ensure we had a roof over our heads and a stable place to live. I was more than willing.

Seemingly, life was starting to have its challenges. But just like my mother, I was going to push through. I decided that my boyfriend's inability to remain faithful was the very last draw. The red flags were flying so high in the sky you'd think the National Weather Service was involved. Certainly the risk of high weather and strong winds increased the risk of fire danger, and not the good kind of fire. No, there was no passion involved here. I had enough red flags at this point. How did I not see it coming? Some men have the uncanny ability to disguise themselves, making themselves out to be "prince charming." They wine and dine you. They tell you all the things you want to hear, and this makes it all the easier to fall. I'm not hard on myself about my lack of maturity. After all, I understood later that this would not only come with time, but with relationship experience. One thing I adopted from my mother though, I will not stick around to be anyone's fool. This too being something I had to learn to move past later on in life. In this moment, however, I was ready. I understood that there really was nothing that would change this man if this was how he was carrying on now. Leading women on and showing no consideration for the fact that his girlfriend was also the mother of his one and only daughter, a toddler still. I didn't look back. And I was one hundred percent certain it was the right decision.

I didn't miss him one bit. In fact, college life was occupying the vast majority of my time. I continued to focus on my studies, though admittedly it wasn't easy. There were so many distractions, I felt like I was robbed of my time in those few months we dated. And now I was on a mission to get my joy back. I felt depleted. Discouraged. Embarrassed. Just plain dumb. Yet, just like in any good Romcom, in came my friends. My girlfriends were a staple during this period of my life. There were endless nights of partying, and yes . . . that also meant drinking. Late nights, early mornings, and exhausted moments in front of the computer where I was working on term papers, studying for exams, and catching up on things I had left for last minute. It's as if I was on a fast-track, catch-up session of the "college life" I hadn't enjoyed. It was the first time I had experienced a lack of interest in school. This was new for me. I started to wonder if I even wanted to finish this program. Was I on the right track? Did I need to take a break? But the thought of it delaying my graduation goal loomed over me. Ambitious plans for this now twenty-year-old started to look less promising as the days went by. I went back and forth about this for a few weeks. And then . . . this happened.

Chapter 9

DEAR MAMA

As if I needed one more monkey wrench in my life's plans. I came to notice that my cycle was more than the regular four months late. Being late was not irregular for me. In fact, that was my "Normal" cycle. It was not uncommon for me to go up to four months with no period. But four months and one day? That was peculiar. The last thing I needed was an unplanned pregnancy, but boy oh boy, did God have other plans. I set an appointment at a local Obstetrics and Gynecology practice. First time in this office, in fact. The office was cold, bleak, and sterile, at best. Adorned with faded maroon chairs and coffee tables loaded with tons of medical brochures, I walked into your typical office waiting room. I don't recall seeing anyone else waiting that day. Then again, I was focused on the front desk where I went to check in. I nervously picked up the black chained pen adhered to the counter and wrote my name on the waiting list. With anxiety, I find a seat before being called back up again. I was eager. I didn't have a regular OB/GYN, though I should have. I thought this should do for what I needed. Crazy how I could have easily just gone to the local pharmacy and picked up a pregnancy test if pregnancy is what I was expecting. But no, it wasn't what I expected at all! My ex and I had been broken up for four months now. There's no way I thought. At least, that's how I processed it. Surely, there was another more serious medical issue I was experiencing.

I walked into the doctor's office not in any way nervous but concerned. The doctor came in and asked me a few questions. In this barren office, I sat on the medical table, answering every question with certainty. Irregular cycles were at the forefront of my mind for the cause of this menstrual cycle delay. Handing over a sterilized plastic cup, he asked me to give a urine sample. I gingerly stepped down off the patient bed and walked quickly to the restroom. I returned to the room, urine sample in hand, covered by a paper towel, meant to provide this part of me a little privacy. With the paper towel draped over the cup like a curtain, I placed it on the table. The nurse came in and used a mini dropper to squeeze a few drops of urine onto a small rectangular stick. I'd seen pregnancy tests before. They were long and had a little window on them where you could see either a plus sign (+) or a minus sign (-) and sometimes even the words, PREGNANT or NOT PREGNANT if you could afford the more fancy ones. This wasn't that. So I knew she was checking for some other more serious matter.

Surely this was a "why do I have an irregular cycle" detector. A more serious condition related to a deficiency—maybe. But I was sadly mistaken. It was exactly that, a pregnancy test. The nurse told me so when I asked. I didn't even know what to say. My heart started racing at this point and I could feel the blood rushing up to my cheeks now. My face felt like it was on fire. She excused herself as she walked out of the room, then returned with the doctor. She had quite the poker face. The doctor held no punches. Upon looking at the stick, and picking it up with his fancy latex gloves, he turned it around and showed me. The next few words coming out of his mouth would be a blur. He said, "Well, you're pregnant! This is the reason for your late cycle."

I looked at the nurse, who, at this point, made intense eye contact with me as if she knew I was about to go into a full-blown outburst of tears. And it happened. The tears came streaming down my face like Niagara Falls. I was overcome with confusion, fear, concern, and worry. The doctor assured me that it was okay. That I wasn't the first, and I wouldn't be the last. He went on to express the next steps in this process, giving me the understanding that I must now begin a prenatal care regimen since I was already four months along. Wow! FOUR MONTHS!?! Like, how did he even know that? I started to calculate in my head how that was even possible. I was so far removed from my ex, I didn't even recall having been intimate with him almost immediately before we broke up. It was a pretty abrupt breakup. But this was now my reality.

Now more than ever, I came to realize that I had only myself to depend on. Or that's how I looked at it, anyway.

It was my responsibility. It never crossed my mind to terminate the pregnancy. Even under these circumstances, I saw this as a blessing. Yes, after the tearful display of emotions, I remembered whose I was. The timing may have been totally off, but as I'd been accustomed to believing; God makes no mistakes. I soon came to see just how on time my blessing would be. I sat there listening to the nurse rattle off my prenatal instructions, but I was totally tuned out. On and off, hearing every four words she spoke. "This is what *you* must do next . . . schedule your prenatal appointment . . . take these prenatal vitamins . . . don't worry, *it will be okay.*" And so it was time to take off this paper gown and put my clothes back on. Slowly placing each item of clothing on my body as if I were now fragile. Because in fact, I was. 'I have a little being growing inside of me,' I thought. I processed this for a few minutes between exiting the exam room and walking to my car. And then I said to myself, "I've got to call and tell him. The right thing would be to let him know." So I did. I drove to the nearest payphone (if you're not familiar, given our advancement, these were public phones on street corners). I rummaged in my car's ashtray for enough coins to make the call. And I did. I made the call.

Surprisingly, he answered. Nonchalantly and in the most matter-of-fact way I could, I told him. "I just wanted to let you know I am pregnant. I don't want you to worry about anything regarding the baby. I will take care of it. I will not be calling you for anything, no worries. I just thought you should know." Silence followed. Crickets. And so he asked, "What are you going to do?" Without question, I was going to have this child.

Whether he was in agreement or not, it was happening. And I never looked back.

The doctor's office was only a short eight to ten minutes from my house. On this brief ride home, I tried to compose myself as best as I could because I knew I'd be walking into the home where my mother could immediately sense if something was wrong. 'Mother's intuition.' I thought. She seemed to have some sharpened antennas. She was the biggest of worry bugs and, yes, I get this from her too. But she was also my mother, and this meant that her maternal instincts kicked in almost immediately as she saw me walk through that door. I strolled into the kitchen, toward the table, and sat down. I asked her to do the same. She asked me again, *"Que te pasa* [What's wrong]?" Why my initial thought would be that she'd be mad at me, I don't know. Somehow, I thought she'd be disappointed. With all that we've been through as a family in the last few years, the last thing I wanted to do was disappoint her. Remember, it's been my life's mission to do the complete opposite. To make her proud. To bring her joy. To give her one less thing to worry about. And here I was about to deliver some news that would change our family dynamic forever.

"I don't want you to be mad at me, but I have something to tell you," I said in Spanish of course. Now would be a great time to explain that, although we've been in the United States for a little over sixteen years by this time, my mother was still not fluent in English. She was eager to hear what I had to say. The worried look on her face made me nervous, but I summoned the strength, by God's grace, and spilled the beans. *"Estoy embarazada,"* I said as my voice quivered. Holding back tears as I sat there, with a knot now forming in my throat like I'd swallowed a dry piece of bread. Her reaction was not at all what I expected. She responded, "Is that it? You are not the first, and certainly not the last." Sound familiar? The very statement spoken to me by the nurse when the doctor shared the news. And it was in this moment that I felt empowered. She's right. I had some personal experience with this, as my sister had just had a baby. I, clearly, was not the first. And I can only imagine how many more young women were experiencing this exact same thing at that given moment. I cried it out in my mother's arms that late afternoon. As night fell, I was changed. I literally was now a different person. 'Nothing would stand in the way of providing a good life for this tiny blessing,' I thought. Once a struggling college student lacking motivation and looking to quit, now a strong, determined, pregnant young Latina with a strong maternal figure to back her up. Failure was never an option.

And so it was. I carried on now with more of a reason to finish school. Imagining plans for the future and timing was everything. An opportunity to purchase *my* first home came up, and you better believe I jumped on it. I began to imagine all the ways I'd make this home ours. *Me and my little one, living life lavishly in our new townhome,* I thought. Because apparently, at this point, I had dreamt up such a successful future. Seeing this structure in person only solidified these plans. As the real estate proceedings began, I continued with my schooling. Focused.

My ex was now determined to make me change my mind. He carried on with his reasoning for why it just wasn't a good idea for me to have this child. It was too late, though; I was committed. Not that I considered it in the first place, but what would possess him to think that I would even entertain his requests? He went heavy on the harassing phone calls, to the point where I asked my mother to screen them. And then the calls stopped shortly after six months of pregnancy. It was a weight lifted off my shoulders. I didn't need the stress. I had enough on my plate. I remember this time like it was yester-day. I was in my bedroom lathering my growing baby bump with Palmer's Cocoa Butter. My stretch marks growing deep and dark and I was doing my very best to make them non-ex-istent. Ultimately, it didn't help, but Lord knows I tried. Greas-ing myself up like a slippery bowling ball in my bedroom, as I continued with my nightly lathering ritual, I felt free.

Days later, I received a call from the mother of his firstborn. She wanted to know if it was true or if the pregnancy news was simply a rumor. Now in a different place, I was saddened to have to confirm this news to her. I can't even begin to imagine the hurt she must have been feeling. I was over it, but her? She was still in it. The father of her child had now fathered a child with another woman. My heart broke for her. But I assured her I wanted nothing to do with him, hoping that someday in the future he may want to establish a relationship with his child, but not at all holding him to it. He would hold that position if he would commit to it. I didn't want my child to experience the kind of hurt a child feels when their "father" doesn't hold up their end of the bargain. I'll never forget the few choice words he did express in the midst of those harassing conversations. Words that would haunt him forever. "I don't want my child to grow up with issues. Kids with no fathers grow up with all kinds of issues." I affirmed to him that I was certain God would place in my life the man that would not only be a father to him, but that would show him he was loved and special. Wait 'til you see how that came to fruition.

Crazy how the mother of his first child and I went from a volatile relationship to one of motherly concern. Our instincts now were to protect our children. For her—to work her way through a relationship that was hard to let go. They had a history, and I understood her pain. She would often tell me, "I wish I had your strength." And so I prayed for her. More now than ever. I prayed.

Months passed, and I grew bigger and bigger by the day. Wobbling my way to and from work, to and from school, until I couldn't any longer. By now, the pregnancy was nearing its most uncomfortable stage. My mother spoiled me with every special craving. Mostly involving fried dough, rice, beans, and chocolate. Most of which I only enjoyed for a short period of time after ingestion as I had developed morning sickness, but not just in the morning. No. The sickness would reveal itself at all hours of the day. I called it "morn-noon-night sickness." It was so severe I wasn't gaining any weight. I'd have to tough my way through it, praying that some food would stay down long enough for me to digest it. It never did happen. Instead, this just became my new normal. My morning routine was hot chocolate and crackers for breakfast. Somehow, drinking something hot seemed to help soothe the nausea, but not always. Making me regret quite quickly that I had consumed it in the first place. There were many days I had to stop on the side of the road midway to my job. Pulling over for some relief. Not pretty, but necessary.

I continued to work at the telecommunications company. Much more at ease now since my ex moved on to other employment. This eased my frustrations; it was a welcomed surprise. Work, school, and home comprised my schedule. Day in and day out, I showed up. No excuses. No exceptions. Until that is, I no longer could. I vowed to work until the very last day. Knowing that I didn't have many maternity leave benefits meant I had to preserve as much time as I could. When the time came to slow down, by doctor's orders, I did.

Chapter 10

ALL THINGS NEW

During my pregnancy, I was also nearing the end of the school semester. Preparing for finals and studying was my normal routine outside of work back then. It was also time to select the courses for the following semester. Coincidentally, spring break was coming up and the timing couldn't have been more perfect. I boldly walked into the registrar's office with my selections. The staff looked at me like, "Are you sure you can do this? Aren't you about to have this baby?" And I, with my head held high and shoulders back, smiled and confirmed what they had been thinking. "Yes, I am, but I'll be ready to take on the next semester by then." So I did. I sat before the registration representative, wide-legged and breathing heavily as I lowered myself onto that seat, then I read off my selections. I could see the look of admiration on her face. For a slight second, I questioned myself. Can I actually do this? *Yes, I can.*

News about my property purchase was starting to frustrate me as the process kept dragging and dragging. I wondered if it was a sign to just let it go. Every day was a new delayed development. The closing date kept getting pushed back further and further. At the "final" closing date, I had already made a purchase for furniture to be delivered. The last straw was when the delivery was shipping out as scheduled and the closing date was again, rescheduled. I had no choice but to terminate the contract. It just wasn't meant to be. The house didn't happen, and I took this as an opportunity to look for new employment. Surely there had to have been a reason for this right?

One thing is for sure, the belly kept growing and time kept keeping on. What I was about to experience would change my life forever. Did I even have expectations? I recall being told by many a mother throughout my pregnancy how each pregnancy is different. What's smooth sailing for some can be complicated for others. So I was open. Open to this new experience. Yes, there were days I wish I had a partner with me to experience these firsts. The first movement, the first kicks, the first sonogram, the first gender reveal, all of it. By my side, each step of the way, was none other than the matriarch of my family. My mother, the rock. The fortress that was the protection for my sisters and me. No one was more qualified for this role at this moment. And I wouldn't have had it any other way. She prepared me. Both emotionally and realistically. Though she couldn't prepare me for the hardships, it was clear that the woman she had raised, the one about to birth this baby, was as strong as her. The true example of what I had witnessed growing up. This was yet another stepping stone to life. Not a failure, another accomplishment. I can do this. And I will.

So even though the little one was delayed in coming, as the days passed beyond my due date I became increasingly anxious and all the more uncomfortable. Needless to say, I wanted him out! Yes, it was a boy. Perfect for me, I thought. What would I possibly do with a little girl? Growing impatient, I tried many home remedies to accelerate the birthing process. Each day, we'd receive a new visitor in our home, a friend of the family, with new methods to try. We walked, we ate, we danced, we jumped, we consumed natural teas, spicy foods; you name it, and we did it. Until the day finally came. The final remedy actually worked. And so . . . at about 3 a.m. on April 1, 2001, I awoke with an intense need to use the restroom. Shortly after, I felt sharp pains. I breathed through them, getting up slowly each time so as to not disturb everyone else in the home. My younger sister slept soundly in her room while I shared a bed with my mother. She wanted to keep a close eye on me given my condition. She briefly woke up when I first got out of bed and asked if I was okay. I confidently advised her I was fine. But I never came back to bed, and she fell back asleep. The next few hours would follow a triggering of contractions. I calmly sat on the living room recliner with my stopwatch in hand. And by stopwatch, I mean my beeper. Remember those? Yet another blast from the past. There I sat, timing the contractions. One after another, I breathed, and I timed. In through the nose, and out through the mouth. I breathed, and I timed. Sitting in the dark, I prayed through it. 'Was it finally time?' I thought.

I recall my OB/GYN telling me I'd know it was time when the contractions were at least three minutes apart. So I waited. And I waited. And waited some more. Until I could see the sunrise from the living room window. Staring into the distance, I couldn't help but wonder how my life was about to change. How this was going to be one wild ride, but I was made for this. I was prepared. My little sister woke up to get ready for school. Seeing me sitting in the living room in total darkness, she jokingly asked why I was "sitting in the dark like a weirdo." She was so loving (I laugh here as her humorous commentary was one of the things I admired about her the most). I calmly said, "I think I'm in labor. My contractions are three minutes apart. But I wanted to make sure it wasn't another Braxton-Hicks scare before I woke Mom up." She immediately said, in full-blown panic mode, "What?! Why didn't you wake us up? I'm going to tell Mami!" In complete disbelief, she ran frantically toward the room to get my mother out of bed. And so it began; everyone in the house was in complete hysteria. All except for me, of course. Calmly getting up from the recliner, I showered, prepped my hospital bag, and we scurried on out the door.

Considering it was April Fool's Day, it was quite difficult getting others to believe I was actually in labor. I don't know why. I wasn't much of a prankster. Maybe the continued failed efforts to trigger contractions before were signs that this was yet another one of those times. Until it was no longer a joke. This was happening, people. My best friend and cousin rushed to the hospital to meet me. My mother, unable to watch me in pain, opted to stay out of the delivery room. In fact, she left the hospital altogether. Something about seeing her daughter in pain and not being able to do anything about it was simply one of the hardest things she had to do. I didn't hold this against her, as it was the same with the birth of my niece. My sister's birthing experience being very traumatic, my mother didn't want to go through this again. She knew her limits, and she knew I was in very good hands. She, the strongest woman I've ever known, didn't shy at admitting that this was just one area of strength she could never master. I would find this out as well in my journey through motherhood.

After being checked in to Miami Jackson Hospital Maternity Annex in Opa Locka, Florida, I started the descent into labor. Not as quickly as I thought it would be, however. In my mind, I'd show up at the hospital and check in, everyone would be in a panic, they'd wheel me to the delivery room, I'd get hooked up to all the monitors, breathe through the contractions a bit more, get my pelvic exam to determine if I was ready to push, they'd give me the epidural, and *bam!* The arrival of my prince. Just as you'd see in a movie. But *nope*. This was no movie. It didn't quite pan out that way. Morning sickness arrived like clockwork. With a bag in hand, I walked the hospital hallways, stopping for contractions, breathing, and getting back to the walk. Finally dilating enough to be forced to lie down and be monitored. Breathing some more, I handled each contraction like a champ. Until the nurse came in and asked if I wanted the epidural. I had heard so many horror stories of women who had gotten the epidural too soon and had delayed labor, causing the epidural to wear off, of moms having to give birth without it for fear that another dose would cause harm to the baby too close to delivery. I definitely did not want this, so I toughed it out. The nurse came back, asking at least two more times if I was ready. Until she gave me no other option. Walking into the room, the soft-spoken nurse tip-toed back in for another check of the monitors. Calling the doctor in for another pelvic exam, she went on to say, "Your uterus is getting tired, and I think now is the time." I hesitated once again, expressing my concern, but she only said, "it's time!"

I sat up as instructed, not concerned at all about the size of the needle or the aftereffects. I did as I was told. The nurse stood in front of me, holding me firmly and giving me *strict* instructions not to move or I would face paralysis. I did (you guessed it) *not move*. Needle in hand, the anesthesiologist was behind me ready to do this thing. I felt a small pinch, and the next thing I knew, I couldn't feel my legs. So I lay there, as I watched my young doctor request the NBA All-Star game to be displayed on the TV monitor. A basketball fan myself, I understood the importance of this, but in this moment, I was a bit taken aback. Like, is he serious right now? My mother called my best friend and cousin for updates on the labor and delivery process. My older sister had recently moved out of town, scoping out new living arrangements with her boyfriend. But she had made her way back to town for this moment as well. Everyone was well-informed. And then it was time. In between pushing, the tempers in the room began to flare. Frustrations mounted between the head labor and delivery nurse and my best friend as the instructions on how and when to hold my leg become confusing. I noticed the concern my best friend had for me and how seriously she was taking this role. After all, it was her godson who was about to enter the world. And I, her best friend and sister could only lay there in a vulnerable position. Promptly, they amicably resolved their differences just in time for the final push.

And there he was, all of six pounds and seven ounces of him. A bright pink baby boy lay on my tummy, ready for the umbilical cord clipping performed by none other than my loving cousin. My Angel, making his arrival into this world. He was healthy and adorable and had more love waiting on him than he'd know what to do with. I was exhausted; nonetheless, I was filled with hope, joy, and myriad other emotions, which I couldn't put into words. I was officially a mother and a boy mom at that. We'd have so many things in common. A proud tomboy, I was eager to show him the basketball ropes. We'd have so much fun. I was truly blessed. The days to come would be filled with an unexplainable light. The kind of feeling that makes you think you were walking on clouds. Now focused on one thing only: him. And all the things in my life he would now impact. The changes to come for the betterment of our lives together. A lifestyle shift like I had never seen. And so it was.

After a brief stay in the hospital, we were ready to go home. All the delicate clothes I had packed in his diaper back for this moment finally found their way to this adorable infant model. He was smaller than we expected, so all his clothes were far too big for him, but he wore the traditional Latin garb as I had envisioned. With him in my arms, I proudly walked out of that hospital accompanied by my mother who was just glowing with pride. As we entered our home, we discovered that my mother's (primary) bedroom would now provide our new sleeping arrangements. While we were in the hospital, my mother made sure to get the crib set up in that space, as it was the only room in the home that was big enough to hold both his sleeping quarters and mine. The crib was adorned with all the gifts that had been dropped off for him while we were in the hospital. It was heartwarming to see how many people were anxiously awaiting his arrival.

My postpartum journey began at this moment as well. The hormonal ups and downs and the leaking breasts that provided his sustenance were quite a challenging experience. It was new to me. Truly a foreign concept. But I was built for this, right? Breastfeeding was a task, yet I was determined to succeed at it. It proved to be so much harder than I thought. How is it possible for something my body is designed for to be so difficult to accomplish? I felt broken, flawed, worthless for not being able to perform the most important task as a mother, to naturally feed my child. As it turns out, it's one of the biggest struggles mommies face post-birthing, right next to postpartum depression. And I was warned of these hormonal shifts that could cause feelings of worthlessness. I braved through it though, determined to do my very best. After all, the show must go on. Day by day, I started to get used to this new life. I marveled at his little face while he slept. And in those moments, when he was sound asleep, I brainstormed. Building a better life for him became priority number one.

Chapter 11

THINKING OF A MASTER PLAN

In the age of dial-up internet, I recall sitting in front of the computer in my cramped bedroom at my mother's house logging on to the internet to search for work. I accomplished this between feedings. My daily routine during maternity leave and break from school was to wake up, feed, pump, eat, search for employment, and repeat. Somewhere in there, I got some shuteye. But not much as you can imagine what it's like to be the mother of a newborn. Sleepless nights and high emotions are due to fluctuating hormones as they settle down from the rollercoaster of pregnancy. Nevertheless, I was determined. I even managed to get some exercise in during the baby's naptime.

As I neared the end of my college career, I figured it would be a better time than any to start establishing some connections in the field of justice. A contract-employment opportunity was available working with what was then the Department of Treasury. This job meant major bonus points for my resume and another chance to prove my skills in leadership. As lead data entry transcriber, I'd be responsible for a team of four, myself included. Small group, major responsibility. I applied and, low and behold, they were thoroughly impressed with my management history. Locking this job in was a major win for me. It meant the start of something new as I worked on finishing school, and it gave me something to look forward to. The possibilities were endless!

The semester was about to begin, the start of my last year in college. My new routine . . . wake up, pump, feed, leave my mother instructions for the baby's care (not that she needed it, but I was very involved in every aspect of my son's life), off to the new job, back home for pumping and feeding, a quick bite to eat, then back on the road for my evening classes at the college. My days would end at about 11 p.m. I treasured every moment I could hold my son during this time. Thus, as you can imagine, causing him to develop some bad habits. My need to hold him and spend time with him soon created for him an expectation that he was to be carried all day long. For you mommies out there that know where this is going, this caused some very frustrating moments. There were many days in which I'd try to get homework done, do chores, or simply have dinner, when the little one would scream at the top of his lungs, looking to be held. I created a monster. Boy, was this a challenge. Then, I had the genius idea to place him in his swing set as the floor bouncer was no longer working. For those new-age parents out there, no, this was not a press-the-button-and-walk-away kind of contraption. This was old-school; crank it up manually until it didn't turn anymore, then walk away and time the end of the swinging before it starts to die down to avoid awakening the baby and causing future screeching. It was the kind of sport you'd have to master—as if you were training for the Olympics. This took precision.

Some days, this process was genius. It worked, allowing me to focus on the things I needed to do and carry on with my plans. Other days, I was *exhausted*. To the point of placing him in the swing and often even forgetting he was there. Mommy-fail. Though I wasn't hard on myself when this happened because he was safe, he was secure, and he was fed. He was simply spoiled. And no, I don't regret it. He seemed to do well with my mother in my absence. I wonder if she too was giving in to the warmth of this tiny body. She never once mentioned it being an inconvenience in her day. In fact, as most grandparents would tell you, it was a joy to have him and provide for him while I was pursuing my collegiate goals and establishing myself in this new career field. She was truly an angel. I don't know how I would have been able to do it without her. It's remembering these moments as a single mother that makes me emotional. Not necessarily because of the difficulties; for me, though difficult, it was something I just knew I had to do. There was no question about it. But I think about the many single parents out there with no support, parents I have helped in my career throughout the years. It certainly breaks my heart, but I have been privy to understanding the various resources available under these circumstances.

The days and months went on, and I had now developed a pretty rocking routine. It was second nature. The most inconvenient of times came when my breastmilk would leak through my breast pads at work or in class, but I always had a backup. Stepping out of the room for a quick change and then getting back to my day like nothing had ever happened. It was my new life as I had come to know it. And, as if out of the blue, I received a call Saturday afternoon from my ex's girl-friend. Remember her? She, quite apologetically and kindly, expressed how she understood and respected my decision to cease communication with the father of my child. Afterward, noting that she was serving as a mediator in this current situ-ation, as he would now like to meet and see his newborn son. I was mildly hesitant but knew that my son was small enough not to be impacted by this union, so I agreed. More than will-ing to accommodate the request. It would be awkward, but I understood it was necessary. After all, he had the paternal right to do so. We agreed on a date and time and eagerly awaited the day's arrival. I informed my mother of this news, and she was in agreement with the encounter. Although, as you would imagine, she was also resistant, given the last few times they had spoken were less than amicable. Still, she was reasonable.

He showed up one Sunday afternoon with a new tone and fresh attitude. He made his way through the white gates that surrounded my mother's house, and I watched him walk to the door. My mother always kept the front door open to get the fresh outdoor breeze. I feel like it kind of reminded her of being back home in the Dominican Republic. Sitting on the couch and watching him walk up, I could see he was nervous. It was a side of him I had never seen before. I looked at him with fresh eyes now. He was now someone I'd be connected to for the rest of my life. Someone I'd consider when it came to making decisions about my child's well-being. Maybe not so much daily consideration as, in fact, I was the custodial parent. And here he was, six months after our last contact, meeting his first-born son for the very first time. I walked up to the door, only a screen separating us at this time. My first fuzzy look at the new father of my child. It was strange, this new place we found ourselves in. Be that as it may, we had a responsibility to our little one. To give him a fighting chance. My mother, standing near the kitchen and dining room area that separated the living room, watched anxiously with protective eyes at the long-awaited encounter while I opened the door and let him in.

Expressing cordial hellos was the least we could do under the circumstances. We were in the presence of a major blessing. Or at least that's how I looked at it. We got right to the matter at hand. I walked him to the bedroom where our little one was laying in his crib. I lifted him up with even more care than I ever had. Holding him in my arms in this moment, I had this maternal overwhelming feeling of fragility. Staring at his rosy cheeks as I handed him over to the arms of his father for the very first time. I wasn't concerned about the way he held him since I knew he had done this before. His beautiful little girl, at this time, was about three years old. He carefully cupped his small round head full of silky brown hair with his left hand. Cradling him in his left arm while supporting him with his right. He looked at him in disbelief. In awe even. At this moment, I couldn't tell what he was thinking, but I backed away, slowly making my way out of the room to allow him some privacy. Being in the same room was awkward enough.

As I watched him from a distance, he began to undress the baby. I observed anxiously as he removed one tiny sock from the left foot, then from the right. Lifting the baby's miniature feet while he lay on his lap, our little boy's back nestled on his father's thighs as his father watched his cute little cooing face. He looked at each toe with an investigative inquisition. Then slowly placed it back down. He moved on to the baby's traditional baby top, a delicate Spanish, cotton, powdered-blue shirt, trimmed in white lace. He slowly undid the tiny buttons on its side and removed the garment, gently and carefully removing one arm at a time then slowly turning him on his side to peer at his back. My eyebrows rose, wondering what he was looking for, and then it dawned on me. Was he analyzing him to determine if the baby was his? Looking at every part of him to see if indeed it was true. This *was* his baby. As a matter of fact, he looked more like his baby than mine. He had droopy checks and a nice white porcelain hue to his face with soft pink cheeks to match. His hair, brown with red highlights, just like his father's and the same ingrown big toe. The only feature of mine nearly recognizable at this time was his cute little button nose. His eyebrows were full and perfectly placed, almost as if perfectly drawn on. His eyes, a beautiful brown color, round and full of life, slightly slanted and meeting at the end, showing some Asian influence. His Colombian roots and my Dominican and Puerto Rican ones shone through. Surely it was the Taino Indian in him. He was clearly a product of our past. A lovely one at that. One that would forever remind me of his father, whether I'd like to admit it or not. That baby was just as much his as he was mine.

Having completed his "mission," he called on me to meet him inside. This time, he spoke in a softer, more appreciative tone. He was singing a different tune, smiling as he went on to say the first few words out of his mouth, "He looks just like me!" I couldn't help but agree. That was truly an indisputable fact. And there would be many years to follow in which he would be reassured even more so. We had a civil conversation, and he made promises he later wouldn't keep. I was hopeful, but I was also realistic. I knew his kind. Charming, positive in the moment, though easily distracted by his own selfish ways. He vowed to see him as the months would go by, wanting to be a part of his birthday celebrations and holidays. I held up my end of the bargain, but disappearing acts were his modus operandi. It was just the way he operated. So I was well-prepared. My main concern was to shield and protect my child from as much hurt as possible. But one thing is for sure, failure was never an option.

Chapter 12

BLUE SKIES

After that memorable first meeting, life went on. I continued with school. Continued with work. And one day out of the *blue*, literally, appeared my "knight in shining armor." I was sitting in the break room at work, minding my business, reading an article actually. Back when reading a physical newspaper was still a thing. I sat there, a party of one, at this cold round lunch table facing the tarmac. Our building was right off the airport runway, so it was relaxing to watch the airplanes fly in and out of the airport. The hustle and bustle of the cars rushing to pick up the imported products which were ready for processing. The manifests shortly ended up at my desk, which I then divided among my data transcribers. Pesky work. Repetitive and yet quite satisfying. I was in my zone. So, glancing up and seeing this gentleman was a great surprise. He was tall, dark, and handsome. He had dimples flawlessly placed on each cheek, and he was well-spoken. This man could carry on a great conversation and was apparently quite impressed with my reading selection. In fact, he used my reading selection as an open invitation to start a conversation. I knew this, but I was intrigued. The usual pleasantries were exchanged. First, there were talks about my professional position. These talks later developed a more personal tone. Then, the next most obvious step was a first date.

He was everything he exemplified. A total gentleman with a lucrative career as a customs agent. Proud of his honorable distinction in his current position and his uncanny ability to detect the illegal ingestion of narcotics in humans as he watched them walk through the Customs gates. This was a skill he later used to his advantage. Months passed as he wooed me. Wining and dining became my favorite pastime next to spending time with my angel. This was something we had in common since he too had a son from a previous relationship. Circumstances similar to mine, though he seemed much more responsible and involved with his child than I witnessed with Angel's father. He was racking up brownie points at a high rate, then came the biggest event to change our world in this country in a way we'd not seen in years.

I recall the events to follow as if it were yesterday. While sitting at my work desk, there were lots of murmurs around me. Shock and despair were the best way to describe it. A plane had just crashed into one of the twin towers. So many questions. My first thought was, 'A plane?' There are planes all around us! Are we safe?! I grew quite concerned and immediately rose up from my seat and walked over to the other data transcribers' desks, informing them of the chaos. We scurried out the door to the breakroom downstairs where we could see the news on the television replaying the crash over and over. The horrific scene, displayed on the TV mounted on a wall in front of the glass window . . . all we saw were airplanes. As we listened intently to this horrid news and the media speculation, we stared at all the planes that surrounded us. As if we had zoomed into our lives, looking from the outside in. It was real. Wondering if we would be told to go home, we stared anxiously at the monitor. Then came another plane. *This can't be happening,* we thought. Goodness! My heart sank. *What's going on?!* It was the question we all blurted out almost symphonically. Shortly after the live footage aired, people began to jump out of the windows of the Twin Towers. I panicked! Relief set in as we got the final word from my corporate administrator that we were to go home for the day. We couldn't exit the building fast enough. *What does this mean?* I thought. I didn't waste any time. I walked back up to my office, collected my things, logged off of my computer, and walked out of the building expeditiously.

On the drive home, all radio stations also reported the news. I just wanted to get home to my baby. As I pulled into my driveway, I remember my mother holding his chunky five-month self in her arms, the sun shining ever so brightly on them. It was a clear sunny day turned dark by the events that had transpired. The terror was stamped all over her face. I didn't even drive all the way in. Just parked the car right at the entrance of the driveway and walked around the car quickly to give them both a hug. In that very moment, we were thankful. Grateful to be in each other's presence. The next hours, days, weeks, and months that proceeded revealed news we never would have imagined. A terrorist attack. And we clearly weren't ready. Finding out about the assailants was beyond nerve-racking. Learning that one of them had visited a private airport just ten minutes up the road made it feel too close to home. It was reported that he had taken flight lessons at this location, gearing up for what no one would ever assume to happen next.

The television was filled day in and day out with scary visuals of the occurrence. From people running away from the ashes that filled the sky to first responders performing life-saving measures on the ones who survived. The tumbling of the towers created yet another rescue mission. The rescue mission which would soon turn into human remain recovery efforts. Truly heartbreaking. I had to turn away from it for my own mental health. Getting news from others as they would share the recent findings was more than enough for me. I had to maintain a positive demeanor in caring for my child. When we got the news that it was safe to return to work, I did. The same with school. Life went on. Now, more carefully than before.

My *blue prince* (we'll call him Ed) however, had to be even more vigilant. Being on the front lines meant he had more work to do. More focus was required. This meant we didn't see each other as much, but it was totally understood. We slowly built a relationship thereafter, committing ourselves to one another as was only natural to do after dating for six months, no? To me, it was a natural progression. Another natural transition was my move toward independence. The time had come in which I was now starting to build a life outside of family. Knowing that I had someone to live for, provide for, and care for, the realization came that I had to do this on my own. I was ready, not to mention I also needed privacy. Long gone were the days of entertaining my date in the living room of my mother's home. Respectfully giving him a kiss good-night at the front door as he dropped me off from our dates. It was clearly time. I don't think she was all too pleased with my dating selection, and I never understood why. There was certainly a shift in our mother-daughter relationship during this time. Could it be that she was starting to feel less important in my life? Sharing this news with my mother was an emotional moment. She was tearful but understood that it was the next most natural step. She gave me her blessing, albeit hesitantly. Knowing, still, that this new journey would require her support. She gave me that, and more.

With my move-in date soon approaching, I began to pack my personal items. Boxing them up a little at a time in order, starting with things I would need the least until move day. Ed waited patiently for the green light. He was responsible for the U-Haul transport loading and unloading of my life. My old life meeting the new—all carefully packed in the back of this five-foot by ten-foot by eight-foot box truck. Enough to fit into a one-bedroom apartment. Though I was moving into a new space, I knew I'd slowly have to fill it with more furniture over time. Baby steps. I had the essentials. The living room furniture (remember that?), the crib, the highchair, my bedroom set (passed on by my mother), and kitchen essentials like pots and pans (also passed down by my mother). I slowly started to buy more things on my own. I'd need a vacuum, cleaning materials, bathroom accouterments, among other necessities. Slowly but surely, my private space was coming together. And I was proud! I had accomplished it. It was *my* place . . . to do as I pleased. Among the most important things about this move was that I could raise my son on my own, with no outside influences on his behavior (no more getting spoiled by grandma) and I wanted to take it all in.

The icing on the cake was having Ed over without the eyes and ears of my mother and little sister lurking behind the scenes. They were a nosey pair. Having the privacy was such a breath of fresh air. But my soon-to-be one-year-old was surely making it difficult. He had become quite attached to me, spending every waking moment by my side with the exception of the times he was with my mother while I was at work and school. He was so dependent that even falling asleep alone in his crib was a non-existent practice. Lord knows I tried. However, I had accustomed him to my bosom. The warmth of my body soothed him and, to be honest, his little body quite soothed me too. We were each other's safety blanket. The whole world could crumble around us, and it wouldn't even matter. I had a little part of me that I'd carry on with me for life. So, yes, I continued to spoil him with love. This meant that weaning him out of my bed when it was time was also quite a burdensome task. But there's nothing I set my mind to that I don't accomplish, so that, too, was successful after some time.

Things were starting to come together, and I had a pretty nice routine going. I'd wake up at 6 a.m. to get ready for the day; showering, changing, and packing my lunch and his diaper bag before I woke him. I got him up and dressed and in my arms with bags and keys in hand by 7:30 a.m. The drive to my mother's house was on the way to work. It took me about twenty to twenty-five minutes in Broward County traffic from Pembroke Park to the city of Miami each morning, assuming there were no accidents or hiccups on the way, leaving me just enough time to drop him off with grandma, say my *bendiciones* (morning blessings) and hellos, and then back in my car by 8:15 a.m. at the latest. Some mornings, our mother-daughter talks took a little longer, but I was sure to make it to work by 9 a.m. I worked my nine-to-five job then hurried home to see the baby and have a quick bite to eat before getting back on the road for my 6:30 p.m. class off Sunrise Blvd, another forty-five minutes from Miami. Then I was done by 9 p.m., heading back to mom's house to pick up Angel and head home. My days ended at 11 p.m. I was exhausted. But I woke up to do it all over again the next day. Monday through Friday, this was my schedule.

Surely, a schedule like this also meant I spent most of my days rushing. There were many days in which I got speeding tickets, had a car accident due to distracted driving (seven in total), or held my notes on the steering wheel as I did some last-minute studying for an upcoming exam. Do not try this at home, kids! Totally *not* recommended. But I saw no other way. My mother would be sure to scold me whenever she could. My time with my Angel was during the week, squeezing Ed in where I could on late nights after I'd put the baby to sleep. On the rare occasion that Ed spent the night, I was adamant about not interrupting my morning routine. He often waited until I was out the door before he exited the room so as not to disturb me. It was a genius plan, and it worked every time.

As the months passed, I received the welcome news that my child's paternal grandmother wanted to meet him. Appreciating family connection myself, I was elated and certainly looking forward to it. In true hosting fashion, I did my best to have the house neat and tidy in preparation for her arrival.

That Saturday, my little one and I vowed to spend some time with his other grandmother, my mother. The one who's supported me through and through in this journey. Arriving at her home on a Saturday morning meant she was already knee-deep in hair clients. One at the washbowl, another in the dryer, and one standing by, waiting for her turn. There was a lot of bickering and gossiping happening in the room as is normal in hair salons. I grew up listening to all sorts of stories, life changes, drama, family issues, you name it . . . I've heard it. It was the norm. Something about the joy of a hair salon and its clients was entertaining. I walked in with the baby on my hip and heads turned immediately. The *oohs*, *ahhs*, and baby talk were expected. He was immediately snatched from my arms by the waiting client, and I said my traditional "*Bendición Mami*" (Blessings, Mother), side-cheek kiss to my mom, leaned over, and did the same with the client in the chair and the one now holding little Angel. Pleasantries were exchanged, and I was quickly ordered to brew some coffee. Being the salon assistant was expected by now. Coffee being a staple in our Caribbean home, I had learned to brew it at the age of six. It was the drink of choice that kept us fellowshipping. My mother drank coffee like water, at least four to five cups a day . . . this was her usual. And still is.

I stayed at my mother's house all afternoon waiting for her to finish with her clients. Some days I'd jump right on in, but on this day, I had things to do. Time with Mom, dinner, and then back home to clean up and prepare for my visitor. Having told my mother who I was expecting, she was overjoyed. Must have been the grandmother vibe. She, more than anyone, knew the importance of a grandma-grandchild relationship. It was an honor bestowed upon her that she was quite passionate about, so she hurried me along after dinner, ensuring that I had my apartment ready, spick and span cleaned for the arrival of Angel's paternal grandmother. This was serious. So, I took on the challenge. As the sun began to set in Miami, I knew it was time to head back; my mother never missed an opportunity to send me home with food. I packed my diaper bag, did a quick bathroom run, and prepped the little one in preparation for our drive home. Weekend traffic was expected. After all, if you've ever driven on Interstate 95 in Miami on a Saturday evening you'd know; it was just as busy at this time as it was during rush hour traffic on a Monday.

As we said our "farewells." I noticed a certain melancholic vibe with my mother. My little sister, just arriving from her job at the Opa-Locka/Hialeah Flea Market, said her hellos and greeted Angel. This bought me some time to pick my mother's brain because she was very secretive. Almost as if she didn't want to get into it, but I knew by now what this meant. My brother was starting to relapse again. Yet another time in her life when she'd have to concern herself with his care. We

spoke briefly about the new turn of events, about his struggles, about her need to get to the Dominican Republic and see
him out of another conundrum. I supported her just as she had
done for many others throughout my life. I assured her that I
would do what I could on my end, even if it meant purchasing
her airfare to get there. And I did. One of the many times I'd
do this in the years to come. Now having a child of my own,
a boy at that, I couldn't even begin to imagine not having any
support in a time of trouble. I knew, though, that this was not
the path she'd hoped he had taken in life. So, yes, she did what
she could, but at this point, I began to wonder if she was doing
more harm than good. Her enabling behaviors were starting
to shine through. But who was I to say what was motherly
behavior and what was enabling at this point? Being a mother
at twenty-one, I had a lot to learn. I just stood on the sidelines.
I watched and did the best I could from afar.

Hugging her tightly, I said goodbye to both my mother and
little sister. My older sister was still living in Central Florida
during this time. Things were surely different now. This was
our new life as we knew it. I walked out the front door to my
car and placed Angel in his car seat. Walking around to my
side of the vehicle, I looked back at my mother, who was now
standing in the doorway of the front door. I waved goodbye,
and she waved back. My heart broke for her. I entered my car
and backed out of the driveway, looking at my little one in the
back seat and silently praying that I'd never have to endure that
kind of hurt. The kind of hurt felt by a mother who is helpless
and hopeless, watching as her son continues to go down a dark
and lonely path. The pain you feel when you've given your all

to a human being you birthed and just don't understand how it got this bad. Maybe she'd given a little too much because now he's turned into someone she didn't expect. Outside influences transformed him forever into someone she didn't recognize any longer. A battle he'll fight for many years to come. I just prayed the entire drive back to my apartment. I prayed.

Arriving at our quaint apartment, I walked to my door as you imagine a single mother would; diaper bag on the right shoulder, kid on the left hip, bags in the left hand, and keys in the right. I opened my apartment door and quickly unloaded all the weight. Placing the little one on the carpet and turning back to lock the door behind me. I walked to the kitchen to place the leftover food from my mom's house in the fridge and turned around to look at the mess I needed to clean up. We'd left in such a hurry earlier today I hadn't realized how Angel had left the living room in disarray. There were toys everywhere. It was a small two-bedroom apartment, so there wasn't too much to do. The focus: to clean and tidy up the baby's room and common areas. I did this, looking back every few minutes to see what he had gotten into. Listening to his every move to make sure he wasn't at risk of hurting himself. I did it. By 9 p.m., the apartment was spotlessly clean and organized. Everything was in its place, and now I was focused on getting him ready for bed. A nice warm bath with lavender bubbles would surely soothe him after a busy day. It did just the trick. After bathing him and giving him a nice warm bottle, I laid him in his crib and walked away. Five minutes later, I came back to check on him and he was fast asleep. Mission accomplished!

Days didn't always go this smoothly. In fact, it often wasn't this easy at all. But today, I was grateful! It was one of the few times I got to kick my feet up and sit back. Sitting in the living room, I took the opportunity to check on Ed before bed. Wasn't too much to discuss today. It had been a busy day for us both. After only a few minutes on the phone, I said good night and lay down. Tomorrow was a big day, and I was very much looking forward to it.

I arose early the next day, walked into Angel's room, and checked his crib, hoping to see him still asleep. This gave me some time to get things together in preparation for his grandmother's arrival. He was sound asleep, lying face down in the fetal position. Looking like a true little angel. I slowly tip-toed out of the room with a smile on my face and got things together for the day. Preparing some finger foods to share and putting together some last-minute special touches to the dinner table. Taking full advantage of the little one's slumber, I showered and made myself look presentable. Shortly after, he awoke and was ready to eat. I carried him into the kitchen and sat him on the kitchen counter as I prepped his food. Then, I tenderly placed him in his highchair, encouraging self-feeding, which he miraculously accomplished with very little mess—a mommy win! Followed by a nice warm bath and a change of clothes, he was now ready for Grandma. I splashed him with some lavender-scented *"Para mi Bebe"* baby cologne. If you've never smelled this, let me just tell you, you won't be able to resist smelling their little necks. Such a sweet and soft delicate baby scent.

The timing couldn't have been any more perfect. Not long after I finished, I heard a knock at the door. Looking through the peephole, I saw what appeared to be a five-foot-tall, fair-skinned Columbian Queen. I opened the door excitedly and gave her a huge hug. She was accompanied by a gentleman friend whom I greeted with the same excitement and welcomed them into my home. Leading them to my baby's room, I was eager to see her reaction and his alike. The screech of her voice when she saw this little barefoot boy dressed in a denim overall with a black onesie underneath truly warmed my heart. She immediately picked him up and nestled her face in his little neck. I was nearly in tears.

What a blessing to bestow upon my little one! The love of family. I gave her a quick tour of his bedroom and she was happy to see how well-taken care of he was. I left her in the room to bond with him and went to the kitchen to grab them a couple of drinks. I placed the drinks on the dining room table as I saw her walk out of the room holding him. The rest of the stay we spent sitting on the living room couch and catching up. The visit ended with her vowing to stay and be involved in his life. This was honestly all I could ever ask for; I was happy. If nothing else, I knew that if his paternal grandmother was in the picture, he would always be connected to his paternal side. This would be more of a blessing than I could ever imagine in the years to come.

Chapter 13

LIFE'S LEMONS

And so, life went on. Another thing accomplished, but there was still more life to live. More struggles to face. One weekend afternoon as I was in the kitchen preparing a meal, peeling Yuca (a starchy, fibrous, edible root of the Cassava plant) I had a minor accident. Well, it seemed minor at the time. A true amateur in the kitchen, I nearly sliced my thumb off. Okay, maybe a tad dramatic, but I did. I cut into my thumb a little deeper than the normal superficial cut you expect to experience in minor infractions that occur with your typical meal prep. I panicked, immediately calling on Ed for help. In an instant, he came by to check on me. He was in such a panic himself that he left his keys in the door and rushed into the house, his mother in tow. My hands shaking, I did as he told me to, placing my cut underwater to make sure it was free of bacteria and applying pressure to stop the bleeding. This took some time. The bleeding finally stopped, and I was able to see the injury. I've cut myself before and it didn't look much different. We wrapped it and I went about my usual activities for the rest of the evening, being careful not to hurt myself and to keep it dry. He left for the night, seeing that I could now manage on my own.

Over the next few days, I found I had very little mobility in that finger, which concerned me. I tried to pull my thumb forward as if to give a thumbs up and found I could barely raise it. So, I decided to get it checked by a doctor. The doctor sent me to a specialist who advised that it was clear I had nearly sliced the entire ligament off. 'Wow!' I thought. Now that was DEEP. Literally. I was shocked. He showed me a visual of the ligament injury with a rubber band, cutting it with some scissors almost entirely on one end, leaving a little sliver of a connection and showing me just how grave the matter was. I nearly lost all motion in my thumb. I was flabbergasted. Geez! How was that even possible? A typical amateur move, not knowing how much pressure to apply in peeling. He promptly scheduled me for outpatient surgery and suggested I bring someone along who would help me drive back. I walked out of the doctor's office in disbelief. I shared the news with my mother who informed me that neither she, nor anyone else, would be able to accompany me to my procedure. Being the strong and independent woman I was raised to be, I understood and carried on, yet another thing I'd have to brave on my own. 'I'll be okay,' I thought.

The day came for the surgery, and I was a bit nervous I'll admit. After all, I was walking into this cold outpatient room all by myself. The doctor promised I'd feel nothing. The numbing agent with which I was injected would be sure to do the trick, and it did. They went in with scope and instrument, finding one end of the ligament and the other, then stitching them together. It didn't take long at all. All in all, in about three hours I was done and on my way home. The doctor suggested I call someone to drive, but I assured him I'd be fine. The injury being on my left thumb made it easy to navigate as I'm right-handed. Driving with my right hand was the norm. I just prayed I wouldn't need to brace myself with my left for any reason in this drive; Miami drivers are aggressive. Traffic in Miami as usual was horrendous, and it was taking longer to get to my mother's house. By the time I was more than halfway there, the numbness was wearing off. Fortunately, I was able to drop the prescription medications off at the pharmacy and bear the pain on the way home for some small relief. Arriving at my mom's house, I realized I wouldn't be able to get back on the road to head home until the pain had diminished. Like a little girl, there I was once again, depending on my mother to help me. This was a challenge for me as I was now used to demonstrating that I could do all things myself. But I had no other choice.

That night, I spent the evening being looked after. It had been a while since this happened. Not even post-delivery did I lean on my mother for help. I was used to the usual "woman-up" and bearing my own responsibilities. But this was different. I had to be careful not to re-injure myself. Seeing how it would be difficult to fend for myself and take care of Angel, she offered to keep him that first week until it was time to remove the stitches. It was my first time returning home without him. Entering my apartment felt cold and lonely. The apartment was devoid of the warmth of his smile and the animation of his messes. But this was necessary until I healed well enough to have him back. This also meant I couldn't go to work. I was quite pleased with a leave of absence, though maybe not so much to this extent. And then the scariest of post-traumatic things occurred.

The following morning, as I was in the kitchen preparing something to eat, I heard a knock at my door. Not expecting anyone, I carefully walked to my door and looked through the peephole. It was a Black male, slim and shady. And nothing like Eminem. After his second attempt at knocking with no answer, he assumed no one was home and reached into his pocket. Suddenly, he pulled out a key. 'Could it be?' I thought. Did this man steal the key? In this moment, I was grateful for Ed's quick thinking. The key he left on the door that very day I injured myself no longer fit this keyhole because as soon as he couldn't locate his key, he changed the locks. Thanks be to Jesus for that. I don't even want to begin to imagine what would have happened if he did manage to get in. But I was totally freaked out.

I don't know why my first call wasn't to the police. Instead, I dialed Ed. He was my protector. Not only did he come to check on me, but he also brought a weapon for me. Never had I even held one before. Was I supposed to use it? "For protection," he said. And proceeded to make it his business to show me how to work it. It would serve as a sense of security for me. After all, we later learned that the individual who attempted to get into my apartment lived across the hall and was recently released from prison. What if my son had been home with me? What if he had decided to break a window or the sliding glass door to get in? So many what-ifs started to roll through my mind. I hung in there as long as I could, never telling my mother about the scare to protect her from her own sense of worry. I didn't want her to think I couldn't handle myself. Didn't want to give her one more thing to stress over. After all, she had more than enough to worry about with my brother and older sister.

I braved the next few months in a state of paranoia, questioning whether he would come back. Lost in a trance of thoughts, 'Would he tackle me as I was trying to get into my apartment? Would I be able to call for help? Would I be quick enough to grab my weapon?' So many questions. So many concerns. Once I was in my apartment, I felt safe. But it's no surprise that, once my lease was up, I decided I was not renewing it. I had to find another place to live. In the meantime, I hesitantly returned home to live with my mother—only for a brief moment, as it was clear she was disliking my boyfriend more and more these days. Her reasoning, she just sensed that he was "no good." A premonition, if you will. Not at all acknowledging that I disagreed wholeheartedly. But she didn't see how he was caring for me and looking after me. I held those things from her because it would mean I'd have to share my most recent traumatic experience. A pandora's box of issues I didn't want to uncover. So I just shook my head in disagreement.

As the days went by, things were becoming more and more uncomfortable between us. It was as if there was a switch I just couldn't comprehend. Like, it's me . . . Linmary! The one who's had your back all my life. The one who's done everything in her power to make you proud. The one who's held back from experiencing life to the fullest because she didn't want to disappoint you. Who's even sacrificed her own happiness for you? But not this time, and I was shocked. For me, this cloud of tension was coming out of left field. So yes, if she didn't like Ed, that was fine...but why be so aggravated with me? I simply did not understand it. And soon she was becoming short-tempered with Angel. Noting that her "nerves" weren't up for babysitting him anymore, I had to find a new sitter. Luckily, I received a referral from a family friend just around the block. Someone I could trust to stay with him, whom I knew came well recommended. Though it was a blessing to have found another sitter, it still hurt. I needed my mother's support. One evening, as the accumulation of disappointment grew, we had our first blow-up. The argument of all arguments sparked my desire to leave. Not knowing where I was going, I walked out of the house just to clear my head. I called on Ed for help and direction, and I found he had an option. This was my out.

It appears he knew of a vacancy in "Little Haiti." If you're not familiar with the Miami area, you wouldn't know that this particular area was occupied by the members of the Zoe Pound, a known Haitian Gang made famous in one of the Bad Boys movies starring Will Smith and Martin Lawrence. I wasn't sure about going to this area, but I trusted Ed. After all, he wouldn't put me in harm's way. Right? One afternoon, I visited this vacant duplex available for rent. In the daytime, it seemed calm. Just a normal Miami duplex with its own private parking and easy to access. It would do, I said, as I agreed to occupy it. It was a studio apartment that would fit my needs and give me back my privacy and independence, so I was all for it. Having had most of my furniture in storage, I moved only the necessities into this space especially since it would be only temporary. I never did tell my mother where I moved and guess what? She never asked. So I took it as a true sign of her detachment.

From that moment forward, I lived my life even more independently. This is when I saw certain moves from Ed that gave clarity to his relationship with the infamous Zoe Pound. This, to me at least, explained why he was so adamant about not being concerned at all for my safety. He knew them. They knew me. And they knew that, in his honor, I was to be protected as well. His moves became more and more secretive. Our relationship? Became more and more estranged. It wasn't long before he started to exhibit signs of disloyalty. Last-minute trips to New York or out of the country became a regular thing. When I asked him what this was about, he was very much "mum's the word." Feeding me very little details of his everyday activities. And some days, he showed signs of worry and stress. But I didn't ask questions. Not long after, it became quite toxic, this relationship. Did my mother see this coming? Toxicity reached levels I could no longer accept. It was starting to affect me. Signs of emotional abuse were first. This abuse lead to bouts of depression and anxiety. The very thing I was proud of, my ability to be strong and independent, had now vanished. Gone down the drain. My mind was battling against me; and, as if I were zapped to another dimension, I became quite a recluse. I knew it was time to get help when I started seeing a decline in my parenting abilities. When endless exhaustion and lowliness meant I forgot to feed Angel and myself most days, I knew I couldn't go on like this.

Speaking to a friend, I was encouraged to seek medical help. When I did, I was not at all surprised to hear that I was diagnosed with Situational Depression. Those two words gave me a jolting sense of failure. My relationship with my mother was "failing." And here I was with another "failed" relationship. This one was different, however, because it wasn't on my own terms. Both fails were like a dagger to my heart. I felt lost, abandoned, neglected, and unappreciated, and I just didn't understand how this came to be. Although I was prescribed medication, I refused to take it. I dug right into writing and used it as my coping mechanism instead. In my mind, taking the medication would mean I wasn't strong enough to get through this on my own. On some level, there were also those cultural influences that just wouldn't allow me to accept meds. So, I did what I do best. I fought my way through it and refocused my attention on the next best thing…a new beginning.

After a few months of coming to the realization that I was about to finally graduate, I started getting my ducks in order. What was next? What was keeping me here? What was I willing to do to get my life together again? The answer to all these questions led to my search for future employment in my career of choice. I was about to graduate from the university with a Bachelor in Science in Criminal Justice so what better time to seek a change of career than now? A job opportunity presented itself within the Department of Homeland Security as a customs agent, which was the exact position held by my now ex. Though it was close to home, I applied. My group of college friends and I passed the written exam, and we were ready to enter the next phase of the application process. It was a blow to my educational ego when I discovered that I hadn't done well on this portion of the process. But I took that as a clear sign that it wasn't meant for me. My job search continued.

Chapter 14

NEW BEGINNINGS

As the graduation date neared, I couldn't contain my excitement. It had been a while since I had worn a cap and gown and walked across a stage commemorating my educational accomplishments. So, I was eager to share the news with my family that my four years of college were finally ending, and I'd be receiving a bachelor's degree. The first to accomplish this in our household! Beaming with pride, I entered my mother's home to share this news one Saturday morning as she was carrying on in her salon. The normal routine on the weekend, cackling of the laughs and women talking over one another was the usual vibe. With clients present and my baby on my hip, I announced the date was approaching. My mother showed pride in front of the clients, matching my joy. She congratulated me as did the women. I showed her my cap and gown, still secured in its original packaging. We talked for a while, then moved on to other more pertinent topics such as hair color and style. After all, she was in her element. It's where I recall my mother feeling most at home; it was her happy place . . . the salon.

The days had passed quickly, and now it was the eve of my graduation. Walking into my mother's home on this fine Friday afternoon, I reminded her once again of the major event. What happened next was completely unexpected. She told me she couldn't make it because there were clients lined up that day and, well, that was a priority over my graduation. I was in complete dismay at the manner in which she communicated the news. So nonchalantly, almost as if she expected me to automatically understand. Now, imagine the look on her face when I expressed my disappointment. This, just one of the many small ways over the last few months that she showed me she was over me. Or at least this is how I saw it. It's simply how it felt. What could I have possibly done to deserve such treatment? Never once did I imagine, in all the years of being her daughter, that she would be so dismissive of something that was so important to me.

This was truly mind-blowing as I thought back to any other moment when I have asked her to be present for me in this way . . . I drew a blank. I was hurt to the core and, after my attempts to convince her of how important this was to me, I dropped the subject. My sisters were also unable to make it. Their reasons, I don't even recall. I immediately withdrew myself from that moment forward. Nothing else even mattered. In fact, as I'm writing this, I sent a message to my girlfriends in my graduating class inquiring if I even attended my graduation. None could recall either. And then it dawned on me: *I did not*. No,

I didn't walk across that stage. No, I didn't get the pleasure of ironing my gown—it is still securely packaged in its original plastic wrap. I kept it and stored it away as a keepsake, a reminder of a very special day for me. A day that I celebrated quietly within myself, as I had become more accustomed to doing over the years. Birthdays, accomplishments, promotions—all were just a part of normal daily living. Nothing special. No grand celebration was required. No balloons, no announcements, no pomp and circumstance.

Nevertheless, it was onward and upward for me. I was focused on moving on and moving up, literally. I landed an interview with an agency contracted by the Department of Juvenile Justice in a Residential Commitment Program for young girls. For this position, I was to travel to Sanford, Florida. My first thought was, 'Where in the world is Sanford?' Turning to my handy dandy dial-up internet service, I pulled it up on the map and found that it was located just North of Orlando and South of Daytona. Nestled right in the middle of these major cities was the small town of Sanford. I was excited to be close to my older sister once again. She had moved up to Orlando and never looked back. She gave me just the encouragement I needed to make the move as well. So I was eager to get to this interview and crush it, as I've done with nearly everything I've ever set my mind to in life. Traveling up the Florida Interstate with music blasting, dressed in my interview attire, blazer propped up neatly on the back of the passenger seat, I was focused. Not nervous at all, having done my research. Not to mention I was filled with all the Criminal Justice knowledge a graduate student could have after completing school. No, instead, I was shining with confidence.

Getting off the interstate and onto the local roads, I entered this quaint little town. The homes were reminiscent of the historic houses I had seen in the movie *My Girl*, with McCauley Culkin (I later found out this town was one of the locations where the movie was filmed). Three-story homes, reminiscent of your typical slave-owner quarters, with wrap-around porches. It's the best way I could describe it. *The closer I get to my destination, the closer I am to my new life,* I thought. Pulling up to this gray three-story home, I thought I was mistaken. In fact, I called the interviewer to ensure I wasn't lost. Was this some kind of joke? I was directed to enter the dirt road leading to the back of the home where I could park and be greeted at the back door. Turns out, the back door was the entrance to the basement part of the home. Immediately, I noticed the cold and drab demeanor of the environment. Steel bunk beds lined up along the walls with their jailhouse mattresses. Artwork was posted up on the walls above each individual bed to mark the territory. I was led to the second level, also known as the first and main living area of the home where the kitchen was. Then up another set of stairs leading to the third level where the offices were located. I was impressed by the layout above. Walking into the front doors of this home, one would never think this was a residential juvenile justice facility. The home-like feel of it, I assume, added to the appeal of the girls, as it made it seem less facility-like and more "homey." Yet it was clear it was nothing like home at all.

After this short tour, I was led into the living area of the residential facility. The room was adorned with what looked like secondhand furniture but was made to feel very much like your at home living room. It was warm and inviting. The walls, lined with house rules and special projects that were up for display for the guests to see. In it, I saw a sense of pride and accomplishment just as much for the residents as it was for the staff. The interviewer guided me to my seat and sat directly across from me. Sitting upright, confident, and at attention, I listened closely to each word spoken to not get stuck on any trick questions, as is a norm with interviewing tactics. I know, I've used them. Having this knowledge made me all the more prepared. One after another, I carefully responded to each question in detail. Eager to share my accolades and experiences. Fresh out of college, I also had a lot of juvenile justice knowledge I could share. And my supervisory experience and attention to detail were sure-fire examples of my case management skills.

Needless to say, that day, I nailed my interview. I sat in the interview chair, gleaming from all the possibilities and thoughts of starting a new life in a new place, which was just what I needed. But I wouldn't be coming alone. Nope. See, in the mix of the graduation excitement, I forgot to mention that I had turned a new leaf on love. Yup, both life and love were looking up for me. Weeks after breaking up with my ex, in the mix of journaling my feelings away, I decided to entertain myself with online dating sites. Having been a loyal AOL customer, I was drawn to match.com. The site matched you up with potential suitors based on your interests. So, I spent a few days perusing the site, just getting acclimated, and I was bold enough to respond to a match one day. That match ended up working for me. This man, whom we'll call Dee, became such a great sounding board for me at just the right time. Our relationship started off simply as friends seeing as how coincidentally we were both in the same place; single and willing to mingle but in no rush whatsoever to commit. As would be the natural progression, this mingling turned into traveling to see one another. The day my son laid eyes on Dee, and Dee on him, was the most magical moment I'd ever experienced. Their eyes lit up as if they were meant for each other. Their bond was immediate, and I was sold!

So back to my job opportunity and the big move to Sanford. Dee lived out of state, in a city he felt wasn't providing much upward movement in his life. Naturally, the move to Sanford would be a great start for us both. What better way to start a new life than in a place that's mutually new? It was an exciting time in our lives. I started the apartment search as soon as I got a start date. The move was happening whether I had a place to live or not. After all, the job wouldn't wait. As a commitment program case manager for a position that desperately needed to be filled, I was eagerly expecting to start training on the date provided. And you know me. Give me a deadline, and I'll make it happen. Having my sister within thirty minutes of me was a joy. I was determined to have my son grow up with his cousins. Every chance we could get them together, we did. This meant taking countless trips to Orlando from Miami in those weeks as I prepared for the move. Having received a move-in date, it was now time to inform my mother. She took the news pretty well. I think the thought of me moving on to take advantage of my degree was a welcomed concept. It was goal focused, and we all know how much my mother appreciated that. Whether she was involved or not, as long as we were pursuing a better life, she was happy. Stagnant living, however, was never welcomed.

Arriving in Orlando, I was surprised, to say the least. I often looked at my older sister as the strong, confident woman I sometimes could not be. I just knew she had her life together. Having spent so much time away from home I imagined she had built a pretty good life for herself. You could imagine how, much to my dismay, I was shocked to see that she had reached a halt in her life's plans. In my perspective, at least, I felt she should have been so much better off by now. By no fault of her own, I believe she was so in love that she was blinded by the possibilities. Though she had always managed to maintain employment at some pretty good agencies, she was not using her degree to benefit her in her current position. It saddened me a bit because I knew just how much potential she had. But it was too soon to tell if that would be something she was going to settle for. I only hoped that, living closer, we would be able to build a stronger sister-to-sister connection. Having been informed by the apartment leasing office that the apartment wouldn't be ready when it was first predicted, I worked out a plan B. My sister agreed to allow us to crash at her place pending the availability of our apartment. This wouldn't take longer than a week or two at most. All was set.

Cue the disappointing mellow-dramatic music here. I was welcomed at my sister's house with the news that they were in the process of vacating their home. The reasons, unknown. And I didn't bother asking. Whatever it was, it was none of my business. Though it would have been nice to have gotten a heads up, considering I was in a new city. So what do I do now with no other place to go? My sister told me she was looking to stay in one of those "pay by the week" hotels up the road. I was skeptical about them, to be honest. They didn't look very clean, but what other choice did I have? I called my mother in a blind rage at the position my son and I were in.

Providing a safe and stable environment for my child was my utmost priority. I had arranged that, and here I was literally homeless. If even for a few weeks. I felt like a failure. Nonetheless, I had no place to call home. After paying for a week's stay and living in this cold and callous room for two days, my mother came along with saving grace. Somehow she had a friend who lived locally and was offering to allow Angel and me to stay there. I didn't know these people. It was awkward at best, but their home was warm, and her friend was so kind. She was truly a guardian angel. The commute to and from work during this time was quite a challenge but the fact that she offered to keep my son while I found adequate daycare was a blessing. I'm forever grateful for this woman in our lives. I learned that my God is an on-time God, and He would never let me fail. Just one of the many times in my life I would recognize this.

And then the day arrived. The apartment was ready, and it was moving time. Dee was given the date and was already on his way to help with the move. My furnishings and boxes were neatly stacked in a storage unit near the apartment. I had strategically organized this on the day of the move to allow a more smooth transition when it was time to execute. Everything was falling into place just as I had planned it. Having him there was such a relief. He and I collectively handled our belongings with care as we moved them in and up the narrow staircase that led to the place we would now call home. It was the first and only time I had ever permanently shared a space with a man. My man. My boyfriend. The experience couldn't have been any more humbling altogether, yet I truly couldn't have imagined going through it with anyone else. My sister had her hands full between trying to find a stable place to live with her husband and now two kids. She couldn't be of much help to us, but it was okay. We knew we'd link up again when we were both settled.

Next up came the search for Dee's employment and my little one's daycare. Daycare was the priority since this needed to be in place before he could start working. For now, they were spending some precious bonding time together. Finding an appropriate facility that would be responsible for our precious cargo was difficult. We toured many daycare facilities of which none met our standards. Dee was as much overprotective of Angel as I was. I'll never forget walking out of one daycare tour in particular where he said, "You've got to be f'in' kidding me?!" and some other expletives I won't dare repeat. It was in this moment I realized that my child wasn't just mine anymore, he was officially his too. We sat in our plainly furnished living room one afternoon and basically agreed to pay whatever it took to get him into the best daycare in town. Just up the road from us was a KinderCare, literally, around the block from the apartment. Every day we'd drive past it, without even so much as a thought because it just looked way too expensive. How would we manage? Dee gave the final word, and KinderCare it was. We would work it out somehow. The child support assistance I received from Angel's father wouldn't even remotely cover the cost, and it wasn't all too dependable, either. So we made the choice, knowing that we couldn't count on that, and it was all on us. Yet, it was the best decision we would ever make.

Thinking back to this period of my life, I don't recall my mother being present at all. Phone calls here and there, yes, but physical presence? No. I was grateful that she was only a phone call away if we needed her, but she had other more important matters to tend to. My brother, for example, on his continued ups and downs with sobriety, and the unfortunate news that one of her siblings had passed away in the Dominican Republic. Another funeral we wouldn't be able to attend. We'd learn that my mother's brother passed away while living alone in a small home he had in the city of El Seibo. The one male sibling in her family had some mental deficiencies yet was somehow able to be independent after the death of my grandmother. We knew it wouldn't be long before he'd pass, as he was very much attached to my grandmother. There were always discussions among the family that he may die of a "broken heart." Many people believe this is actually possible. This could have very well been the case, though the official cause of death was cardiac arrest. We were saddened at the thought of not being able to accompany my mother during this time.

I wondered how she was managing on her own. Was she lonely? Did she need us? Though our conversations had become pretty short and sweet during this time, she seemed to have established a life on her own. The first of many trips we would take down to Miami to see her was the first time she'd met Dee. Immediately, she was pleased. He was such a sweet guy. Though he didn't speak any Spanish, he found some common ground with her. She seemed to thrive on the attention. As a matter of fact, maybe that's why she didn't get along well with my ex, Ed. He didn't really shower her with attention in this way. She was happy—at least, in our presence, she was happy. And so was I therefore I knew better than to touch on the topic of my brother, a sore subject I knew would send her spiraling into a stage of melancholy. One day, however, she reached her breaking point. She had hit her max and changed her phone number. She didn't answer his calls for nearly a year, hoping this tough love would change him. It didn't. I mean, intermittently, maybe. But there were many trips taken from Miami to Santo Domingo, Dominican Republic placing him in rehabilitation facilities, bailing him out of jail, and many other redemptions thereafter. He just couldn't seem to get it together.

I was happy when she finally decided to focus on living her life. After all, we were beginning to do the same. All we've ever wanted was to see her smile, live, and enjoy the fruits of her labor. Now having children of our own, our secondary wish was that she be involved in our children's lives even if she had been unable to be in ours the way we wanted her to—present. This was her chance to redeem herself. The grandkids really did speak life into her when she needed it. We did our best to incorporate her into our lives though, as the years went on, she grew more and more isolated. The rivalry between her siblings and her grew more and more out of hand. My hope was to bring the family together one day, but I knew this would take some time. It certainly wasn't something we could force. She was always headstrong. What she said went. There was no changing her mind. We learned to respect that, for the time being at least.

Chapter 15

STRONG LIKE A BULL

A s the years went on, I grew stronger in character. No longer willing to accept the short end of the stick, I stood up for myself. Both with my mother and in my relationships. My soft spot was always existent, so it took me some time to establish myself in some areas. But when my little sister needed a place to stay, as she was learning to expand her wings and become more independent in the world, Dee and I were honored to have her. It was the start of an eye-opening adventure. By this time, I had a four-year-old while learning to navigate how to guide my little sister, now nineteen years old. And I was certainly up for the challenge. I found that communication was key, and it was the only thing I asked of her as she came and went as she pleased. Creating a communication log for her seemed ridiculous, but for me, it was my attempt at being able to discuss the important things that were happening day to day since we often missed each other in passing. Dee had a soft spot for my little sister, though. The all-too-loving brother-in-law, always giving her the benefit of the doubt. And I, the goal-oriented thinking big sister, needed that balance.

While that season of our lives was challenging, she soon found her own way and officially spread her wings. She had friends and relationships she was building outside of our home, and that was totally okay. I only prayed she was able to continue to grow as she needed to at this time. Even so, I "released her." But really, I was releasing myself from the sense of responsibility I had placed on myself for her success. Plus, I was starting to have my own issues to focus on. Dee and I started to drift apart somehow. In our home, he was the ideal partner. He was an amazing father to Angel, and we got along like best friends, but that's just what it was becoming. We were starting to enter the friend zone. This romantic distance caused us both to drift apart.

I'll never forget Valentine's Day that marked the official breaking point in our relationship. As his phone lay on our nightstand charging, I heard a ping. He happened to leave the apartment momentarily for a late-night grocery run, forgetting his phone, which was quite uncommon. Curiosity piqued my interest, and I looked at the phone. It was a Happy Valentine's Day message from an unknown number. Clearly, this was out of sorts. Who would be sending him such a message on a Valentine's Day evening? Once he returned, I confronted him about it. He brushed it off as if it were nothing to be concerned about, just a friend from work. I recall he had some working relationships he was building at his new job. So I let it go, but I remained vigilant.

Because we shared a cell phone account, one day I decided to check the call log. I noticed there were several calls being made that he was either on his way to work or heading back from work. It was now time to have a more serious discussion about this random number. He, being the true man I've always known him to be, admitted it. He had been having conversations with a woman he met, but it didn't go beyond that. Still, I felt betrayed. Truly beside myself, I was hurt, but I felt it was only a matter of time. Truth is, I couldn't blame him. We were less and less connected, and well, what else was he supposed to do? I'm a true believer that we must fight for our relationships. But the moment you start looking for outside sources to comfort you and provide for you, or even having a simple conversation becomes impossible, it's time to go. So, although he didn't one hundred percent agree with this next step, I moved. It was time to part ways. And this is just what I did -removing myself from situations not fit for me was the norm. But now, it wasn't just about me. My son was also a factor to consider. Angel was so attached to him. I knew this would be hard on me, but I refused to stay in a relationship where neither one of us was happy. Maybe we needed this break. Maybe we moved too quickly. Time apart would be good for us both.

I found a quaint townhome only fifteen minutes away. During this time, my little sister started to come back around as well. She was pretty much living the nomad life, back then, unsure what her next move was, so we agreed to have her stay with Angel and me. Dee, being the gentleman that he was and the only other helping hand I had, agreed to help us move. It was a family affair. In many ways, I knew it was his way of making sure we were okay. Never leaving our side even in the midst of the confusion in which we were living. In this new place, I was most drawn by the lake view. Albeit a manmade neighborhood lake, it provided the solace I needed for the moment. It became the newfound serenity I needed, my safe haven. It was time I considered my next move. All I could think about was making sure my son was okay. I wanted to ensure this transition was exciting for him to distract him from the obvious void in our new home. All in all, I knew he missed Dee.

My sister, a creature of habit, was coming and going as she pleased. And as if that wasn't enough dysfunction, Angel started to have difficulty falling asleep. Bedtime was brutal, night after night of him crying and begging for "Daddy" to come back. "I miss Daddy!!!" he'd yell. It came from the depths of his little soul. The look in his eyes nearly tore me apart. I knew Dee was only a phone call away, so we started evening calls until the calls didn't suffice. As a parent, there is nothing more heart-wrenching than watching your child's heart break for the change in a breakup or separation. I can't imagine the mothers who go through a divorce and how hard this must be for them. I see now why it's so easy to fall back into relationships. Yes, I see, because that's exactly what I did. I succumbed to the need to make things work again with Dee for the sake of my son. An idea I had always been so against in the past, though I would have done anything for the sake of my son's happiness. As for my sister, I spent early mornings with the TV turned on, hoping I didn't see her flash across the news in some kind of car accident. Lord, I was becoming my mother. My patience was wearing thin and one day I simply asked her to go. It was just all too much to handle.

I never thought I'd be that woman, the one who'd consider giving it a second go for the sake of her child. I mean, let me be clear here. Dee was AMAZING. With the exception of the little mishap within our relationship, he was the ideal man. We had a long talk the night we decided to give it a try once more. We spoke deeply about our relationship as it currently was, remembering the reasons we fell for one another and establishing guidelines to ensure we would be successful the second time around. He agreed to give it his all, and I would do the same. Our son, elated. Happy to have "Daddy" back home. The lease on the apartment was up in seemingly perfect timing, and Dee moved into the townhouse. The moment Dee walked through those doors with his belongings he filled the home with love. Settling into our two-story townhome was easy. Our son was eager to spend some quality time with "Daddy" and things were surely looking up.

I couldn't help but wonder at these times how my mother was doing. Though we spoke daily, I was always careful not to express the difficulties we were facing. My goal was and always has been not to give my mother more than she already had to bear. Carrying on the same responsibility I did since I was a kid—it was easy to do. It consisted of omitting information (in my eyes) more than keeping things from her. After all, what good would it do? She'd only stress about things she couldn't control, and I didn't want to hear the bickering. She was always adamant about giving her two cents even when it wasn't solicited. The last thing I needed to hear in this moment was demanding orders from her about how I should have handled things and how she didn't agree with my every move. So keeping things from her became a habit, a way to keep the peace so to speak. In fact, I wasn't the only one. My sisters did the same. It was the necessary evil—dealing with Ms. Linda. For her sake and ours!

During our time living in this townhome, we experienced some wonderful memories, including Dee's mother visiting for our little one's birthday and the start of his first-grade elementary school year. We were excited for him! His little face lit up at the thought of wearing a backpack and going someplace new. I remember it like it was yesterday. Dee eagerly woke him up for his first day just as excited as he did when Angel started pre-kindergarten. Brushing his teeth, singing good morning songs, feeding him breakfast, and dressing him was his jam. He reveled in the opportunity to do so every morning. I watched gingerly from afar, admiring this bond that they had. Calling him "Daddy" came naturally to him after coming home from Pre-K one day and telling us how mommies and daddies picked up his friends from school so logically Dee must be his "Daddy." Considering his biological father was absent from his life, I didn't feel the need to explain it. In truth, by this point, he had not been around enough for Angel to know the difference. I knew it would be my responsibility to explain this to him as he got older. Vowing for it to be an easy transition, transparency was my full intention.

One day, out of the clear blue sky, we received a call from Angel's biological father requesting to speak with Angel. Speaking to him over the phone, however, was a challenge. As you can imagine, Angel had quite a short attention span at his age. This particular night, both Dee and I stood by as he talked to his father. Dee felt the need to support him in this moment and knew the strained relationship we had. I was always very honest not only about my shortcomings but about his as well. The phone call went from calm to irate when his father heard him call Dee "Daddy." His reasoning made no sense to me, as it was completely illogical. I tried to explain that Angel started calling him that on his own, but his father was not having it. He became more and more irate as we attempted to talk some sense into him. It was the ego talking, I know. But the words he spoke to me that evening in rage stuck with me for a long time. For me, it was the turning point of my inability to hold a civil conversation with him. Dee agreed to step in and be the mediating party under the circumstances. Years after, that's exactly how it would be.

It was just better this way, as peace of mind was always important to me. For without peace, I could accomplish nothing. Even with the disagreements between my mother and me, I had to find some peace. Whether it happened by turning a blind eye to her irrational conversations and demands or creating space between us, peace has always been what I sought. This is why it was so easy for me to step away from situations, never allowing myself to wallow in the pit of unhappiness for too long. Was it a coping mechanism? Maybe. But it worked. It worked, and I wasn't changing that anytime soon.

So, as Angel was settling into elementary school, we decided to make a move to a more neutral space. Dee and I started off together in this lone city, then split and ended up in a spot that I chose for myself during that break. We started looking for a new place that would allow our little one some backyard space all to himself, with some privacy. We found a beautiful three-bedroom, two-bath home in a quiet subdivision just minutes outside of town. The home was perfect for us. We were excited to get in there and make it our own. The most exciting of all things was creating a space for our little one. We wanted to make his room fun and give him the world. This was easy to do. My sister had her own space in the guest room because, as you may have guessed, she came back around. Dee was such a sucker for second and third chances. To tell the truth, he just always wanted her to know that it was okay to come back whenever she felt she needed to. Maybe he'd been there and had a special place in his heart for underdogs. I wanted her to know the same, except I was geared up and ready to give a speech in the process. That "big sis to little sis get your act together cause you're getting too old for this" kind of speech. I learned to tone it down though, I'll be honest, and Dee gets all the credit.

Now in this new home, we saw a lot of firsts. Angel's first real accident falling off his bunk bed, which led to a broken arm. Angel's first sleepwalking episodes. Angel's post-soccer tournament exhaustion laid out on the living room couch over Dee's lap. Angel's first pet turtle and the passing of said turtle. And the planning of our "wedding." Yes, we started planning a wedding. His mother was thrilled to have been involved in the process. The only problem here was, he never officially asked to marry me, nor did he present me with a ring. There were simply very serious talks of marriage and engagement. I made calls and picked the wedding colors and the destination, and the bridesmaids were lined up and all. The theme was Tiffany Blue. We just started to feel like this was the next most natural progression in our relationship.

My mother, however, was never a part of these conversations. I can't explain why. Most women would have turned to their mothers first, but it just wasn't the same for me. Was it that we never developed that mother-daughter bond? I knew that, once the details were set in place, she would be more than happy for us to take this step, but planning was not her forte. My mother was just not about celebrations. In fact, I don't believe there's been a celebration up to this point where she was genuinely happy and in the moment. Moments in which we got together were quickly overshadowed by the fact that my brother wasn't around. The happiness of the moment quickly zapped out by her sullen demeanor. So, I didn't feel bad at all for excluding her in this process.

Although, in the wedding planning, maybe I was getting too far ahead of myself because things started to change again. The contracted agency for which I worked was under fire for Medicaid Fraud. Yup, you read that right. An agency working with the State Juvenile Justice system had the gall to steal from the State of Florida and was now forced to close its doors. I immediately started searching for employment elsewhere. Yet, we were bound to carry out the rest of the time at the Commitment Program as there were still juveniles who were court-ordered to complete said program. My responsibility was to ensure that they completed all court-ordered sanctions and made arrangements for transport home once we got the final okay that they were free to go.

A position for a juvenile probation officer was advertised with a local law enforcement agency. The main requirements listed for this position were case management experience and a bachelor's degree; I just knew I had it in the bag. Moreover, Dee encouraged me to give it a shot. After all, I was qualified. About this time, he and I were starting to drift apart as well. Once again, our relationship had transitioned into more of a friendship. If I can be honest, I'd say we'd been in the friend zone for a while now. But he was always so supportive of me and my endeavors, giving me the push I needed to conquer this next challenge, and a challenge it was. I applied for the position, interviewed, and yes . . . got the job. The position required a four-week training in Quincy, Florida. Quincy was located near the state capital. A four-hour drive away from home, to be exact. I would have to successfully complete the Juvenile Probation Officer Academy and "earn my stripes," so to speak. Those few weeks were grueling.

This was the first time I had ever been away from my little man. Knowing that I was doing this for him was the only thing that kept me going each day. I managed to develop some long-lasting relationships from this academy class. We even slipped in a little fun during those weeks especially since we were all in the same boat. Our futures depended on the success of this program and ultimately the passing of the final state exam. I, the class leader, took my position quite seriously. It was an honor to see that, in the end, we all made it through.

The end of the Academy Class meant it was time to officially graduate. A graduation ceremony where many of our friends and family would be present to see us walk across the stage. If you recall, the opportunity I did not have in college, yet it had finally come once more. It meant all the more knowing that my little man and Dee were there to support me. They were the only fans I needed.

Leaving the graduation ceremony that day, I got a text message on my work-issued cell phone from a "Sgt. Green," congratulating me for my accomplishment. I replied to his text message thanking him, then asked another classmate/co-worker who he was. She informed me that he was a new Sergeant in our unit, and we would meet him upon our return to the office on Monday. I was ecstatic to see that this new journey was starting to look like a promising future. Excitedly, I was ready for whatever this position had in store for me. Official certification in hand and dressed in my royal blue gown, I walked back to our sleeping quarters to gather my belongings and meet Dee and my little man for the four-hour drive back home from the Pat Thomas Law Enforcement Academy. Wouldn't be long before our little one was fast asleep on the car ride, leaving me and Dee to have an adult conversation. We both pretty much realized that our romantic relationship was no longer existent, and we started to discuss what life would look like as just friends. Our biggest concern, of course, was Angel. With our lease soon ending, we both agreed it was time for me to start looking for an apartment. We arranged a good schedule that would work for us in the meantime and made sure we put the little one first.

When it was time to move, we made it exciting for Angel. playing on the fact that he would have two special and dedicated rooms to which he could look forward. We each made that space for him extra special. Now about six years old, he understood it a little better. Dee promised to be a part of his everyday life, as usual, giving him the assurance that he needed in knowing that he wasn't going anywhere. There were first-day-of-school meetings, after-school pick-ups, parent/teacher conferences, and school activities—all of which Dee partook. But he didn't stop there. The daddy/son barbershop trips on the weekends continued, as would play time and nights out. It was a smooth transition, and this time around, we were all happy.

Chapter 16
LOVE ALWAYS WINS

Dee had begun dating, and I was happy to see this new season in his life. After all, he deserved happiness, albeit with someone else. He deserved someone who would give him the attention he wasn't getting from our relationship. And as for me, well, remember "Sgt. Green?" Turns out he had his eye on me long before I even knew he existed. Mike, as he would lovingly be known to me, thereafter. He noticed me as the new employee at some point and made it a point to pursue me ever since. I knew nothing about this man except that he was proud to describe himself as the first black sergeant in the agency. I, however, thought this was a bit overzealous; nonetheless, it was certainly an accomplishment in an agency where Caucasians were the majority. His personality reminded me of the comedian Martin Lawrence whom I had a crush on growing up as well. Mike had this sweet and gentle swag about him when we were together, and a rough and tough exterior. Quite like a crab for his Zodiac Sign was also a Cancer. Days of talking and pursuing soon turned into weeks, which turned into months, then turned into years.

By this time, Dee and I developed a respectful and mutual relationship within the scope of moving on. I saw his rise to success within the job he worked so hard to obtain when we first moved here. Seeing it all come full circle and coming into his own was joyful for us both. For me especially, it was prideful considering I could recall the many nights I journeyed to his job, the little one in tow, to pick him up from work at a time when we had to share a car. We saw each other through the struggles so to see each other moving on into our own successful careers was all the more exciting. We deserved it.

Dee's happiness gave me permission to move on and do the same. I felt like I owed him that recognition, if even in my mind. As for Mike and me, we continued to grow in our relationship. We had seen some difficult times through the years. Being twelve years my senior, he came with some pretty hefty baggage, baggage that kept piling on one after another and led to some difficulties early on in our dating relationship. Those circumstantial moments led to our separation in the five years we'd been dating. I also needed to grow.

Angel was starting to grow into his adolescence. By now, Dee and I had a pretty good rhythm with respect to Angel. When his biological father would come into the picture, it was Dee who took on the task of communicating with him. He made himself available for the child exchange, a duty Mike would take on as well. After the last verbal assault by his father, I vowed to remove myself from that position.

In those difficult years with Mike, I sought my mother's love and attention. It was a time I felt alone and needed direction. I leaned on my faith so much so, my faith grew stronger during this time. It being the only thing I could depend on, really. The comfort of knowing that things would be okay was something I longed for. "This, too, shall pass," he reminded me. One of the most difficult times in a woman's life is when she's been betrayed, led astray, and manipulated. My mother, having known this feeling all too well was quite protective. In many ways, her commentary reminded me she was still holding on to parts of her past where she had experienced the same. Her critique was harsh but expected, and this created one downside. When Mike wanted to come back around and "work things out," I had to break down the very walls I had been responsible for causing my mother to build. Heck, I had built those same walls within myself. I knew it was time to seek medical attention when the stress began to cripple me. Fainting spells, fatigue, and yes, depression crept their way back into my life. Now with a new diagnosis; anxiety. I remember thinking, 'Lord, if this is my reaction, how did I never see my mother this way? Did she hide it that well?'

Breaking the news to her of our intention to seek couples' counseling and work things out was not at all what she was expecting to hear. In fact, I waited a little while before I decided to go to her with this tidbit of information. I wanted to make sure that I was making the right decision for myself first, and I was also embarrassed that I needed to have the discussion at all. A few weeks into counseling, both Mike and I were on the same page. We agreed we would take it easy moving forward. A step at a time with no solid decision on whether we were officially together, letting our progress and actions speak for themselves. In other words, we would ride the wave and let the wind carry us where it may. Doing this made it easier to explain to my mother. She wasn't all too content about that, as you can imagine. She was uncomfortably silent at the first mention of it, knowing that it was my decision to make, but all the while feeling like she needed to counsel me. After all, it was that motherly instinct, and this I understood. I imagined that it pained her to see me hurt without being able to do anything about it. All the more, she didn't want to see me make the same mistakes that perhaps she thought she had made in a similar circumstance. This must have been a hopeless feeling, so I didn't hold that against her. I only hoped and prayed that if and when things progressed, she would be open to being more inviting.

And so the time passed. The weeks, months, and years had passed and before we knew it, we had moved into a more solid and healthy relationship. The couples' counseling, faith-based counseling, and church attendance certainly helped. We were in a much lighter and brighter place, and we knew the next best move would be to solidify our union. In time, I also began to notice a change in my mother. She grew more and more distant. I never fully understood why, it just became inevitably apparent. Her focus turned toward my older sister and my brother. Though she did often worry about my free-spirited little sister, she wasn't as involved in her life as much she was with my other siblings. It was almost as if she thought *we* didn't need her too. If truth be told, I recall her saying those words. She said, "I don't love or favor them over you. They just *need me more*." Those five words would echo in my head over the years to come. As our mother-daughter relationship continued to struggle. For me at least, I wasn't so sure she even noticed the shift. I pained for the absent love of my mother in moments I needed it the most. I thought about all the things I had done and sacrificed and the ways I carried on as a child to gain her love and attention and still failed to receive it.

Did I mention how I used to hide things as a kid in order to be revered as the "finder of things" and somehow get that shiny gold star? It felt like then I was able to receive at least the recognition that I deserved. I had to make myself visible. And so I did the same in adulthood, sending gifts religiously on Mother's Day, Christmas, and birthdays and going down to Miami to see her as often as my job would allow. Holding up my end of the bargain as her daughter, and not just any daughter, but a Dominican daughter, who, in my opinion, is required to do so much more. Let me explain. For she and every other Dominican adult that surrounded me in my upbringing demonstrated that it was our responsibility as kids to provide for our parents. I'm not talking about in adulthood here; I'm speaking of a sense of responsibility to our parents as soon as we are able to provide. Providing not only in the sense of being present to show love and attention but also financially. This explains my need to do what I could to help provide for my family the moment I was able to work. Looking back at those times, I wish I had been more like my siblings. They didn't take this responsibility so seriously. They lived their lives unapologetically. They were who they were and asked for forgiveness later.

Over the years, I started to hurt more and more over our conflicted mother-daughter relationship. Feeling as if it was treatment undeserved. It wasn't jealousy, as she'd often like to say; it was a pure and full-blown feeling of abandonment—if we can call it that. I felt invisible. These feelings followed me into adulthood. Some moments felt more intense than others, which resulted in my need to seek an unbiased opinion. A mental health professional opinion at that. Was it me? I often asked myself this.

One of the toughest moments I experienced regarding my relationship with my mother involved her continuous need to hang the phone up on me, a level of disrespect I could no longer tolerate. It was usually the end result of a normal conversation in which I "had the nerve to" (in her opinion) express my feelings. How dare I communicate to her that I felt she was exhibiting enabling behavior? This hurt me to the core. My therapist suggested I write her a letter, and it made perfect sense. In a letter, she'd have no choice but to read word for word how I was feeling, and I'd finally be able to get it all out without the hang-ups. I thought this was a genial idea. In fact, I couldn't wait to get that follow-up call where she'd convey how sorry she was for making me feel this way and at least acknowledge my hurt. Instead, she read that letter and perceived it as my way of telling her she was a terrible mother. Completely flipping every word to a defense strategy. This. This was the moment. The official switch. The setting of the boundaries would make our mother/daughter relationship nearly non-existent.

Chapter 17

GOD'S PLAN

I spent the next few years trying to make sense of who I was. Soul-searching. Growing spiritually and shifting my mindset. I went on to not only marry Mike but also build a blended family. Additionally, I developed a more solid relationship as a blended family with Dee, his wife, their children, and ours. High school years led to basketball activities which pretty much became a part of our daily lives. If it wasn't high school basketball season, it was off-season Amateur Athletic Union Basketball Leagues or volleyball. I turned my attention toward my child in the years I felt he needed me the most. The years when I'd have to be more vigilant and observant, ensuring I guided him through his high school career so he felt supported, loved, and appreciated. We did all that. My mother was never really involved in many of these moments, though I do recall one game that she attended when she came into town to visit my sister. It was definitely one of those types of moments I wish we had been able to share more of, but I took it as it came.

My mother was always so loving and accepting of Dee. It was definitely his kind demeanor that won us all over. So, in her eyes, there was no one who could ever compare. Truly, Dee held that special place in all our hearts, and more so when we learned of his Cancer diagnosis. It broke our hearts. He was only in his mid-thirties. We honestly never saw it coming. Breaking the news to the kids was one of the hardest things I've ever had to experience. The years to follow were focused on his treatment and his well-being. Angel even asked to spend his Senior Year by Dee's side, vowing to be there for him every step of the way. Helping to feed, dress, and administer his medications in the same way Dee had done for him as a child. After all, this was his daddy. The man who loved him unconditionally, beyond measure. He knew nothing else than to pay it back. He deserved every moment. During this season of our lives, both Mike and I would stop by and spend time with Dee as well, including him in our activities. We made it a point to stay connected and help with his stepchildren, as I'm sure it wasn't easy for them to see him deteriorate through the chemo treatment process either. Somehow, Dee maintained a positive attitude. Like the angelic figure he was, he was still present and dedicated to his family. You can imagine my mother didn't take this news too well either. And when he didn't see remission in sight, we all became numb to the process.

I'll never understand why such a loving soul would have to endure such a devastating fate. But I do know that, in my spiritual journey, I've learned some people are sent to us here on earth to show us that good does exist. That there is hope. That God always has a plan for our lives, albeit one we may not ever fully understand, but it is not our job to make sense of His plan. We need only do just as Dee did in this lifetime. Love and care for one another unconditionally. His relationship with his mother taught me so much. He, having been her only child, was the blessing of her life. She carried on through life in this same way. Until his last days, she joked about the fact that Santa was real. He rolled his eyes every time she'd call with what he claimed as "that nonsense." But it was adorable to see that they had a solid relationship. Was it perfect, no? But it was theirs. She understood him in ways no one else ever would. I owed him so much for the father figure he was. For being such a solid and caring friend through the years. Caring for him in exchange came naturally. He deserved every bit of it.

My mother called me often during this time in our lives. Some days it was too much to bear, dealing with her emotional outbursts while I was trying to keep it together for my son. So the boundaries were set. To be honest, her feelings about that didn't matter to me at that time. We had bigger fish to fry trying to cope. In our attempt to help the kids during this difficult moment, we took them along with us on our annual family resort weekend. Throughout the day, I had been texting Dee, checking on him as I usually did. By now, he was experiencing numbness in his hands and having a harder time replying, although it was a bit concerning at first when he didn't reply, I tried to remain calm and understand his current circumstances. Since Mike had to work the last evening we were there, I asked him to stop by his place to check on Dee and make sure he was okay, considering I never got a response. We knew his wife was working all day as well and hadn't been by the house yet, so Mike willingly stopped by. Those next few moments would be a turn of events so drastic and disturbing that they're still difficult to relive.

When Mike walked into the house, he found Dee in distress on the bathroom floor. Immediately, Mike's instinct was to call Dee's wife and 911 to get him to a hospital. He was vaguely responsive, but the doctor made the quick decision to transfer him to hospice thereafter. The time we were so hesitantly expecting had come. These were Dee's last moments. We corralled around him in the only way we knew how. The hospice facility just so happened to be five minutes away from our home. Convenient only because it would allow us an immediate response if things got dire. The doctors kept him comfortable with pain medications—as is the norm in hospice care. The first day or two he was talking, and even walking (with help) to the restroom. The last day before I'd ever hear his voice again he uttered these words, which still ring in my head. I'll never forget, he said, "Why do they keep calling my name?" I responded quickly to his inquiry. "Who? Who's calling your name, Dee? I don't hear anyone calling your name?" And he just reiterated the same. "See? There they go again?"

Later that day, I told my mother about this; and being a believer in the afterlife, she confidently explained that it is common for this to happen, as these were likely people calling him from the "other side." She went on to explain that this happened with her mother and father when they passed and that this was quite a common occurrence in someone's last moments. In some way, her explanation comforted me. The fact that it was my mother who expressed this was also a relief. Her words would always be comforting to me, especially because it wasn't often that I heard them. She further advised that he was being greeted by those who loved him as much, if not more than we did here on earth. Dee was extremely close to his grandfather whom he so lovingly called Paw-Paw, and I know this was one of the angels calling him on the other side. Angel's paternal grandmother, Nubia, was another; although she was not related to Dee, she knew him. Yes, the Colombian Queen was the glue that bonded her grandkids together. I still recall her as soft and sweet as the day I prepared for the initial meeting with Angel in my first apartment. She had passed a year prior due to medical malpractice. Dee also had a child-hood friend he lost not long before, who gave him a warm welcome, I'm certain. Dee was a "collector of people" as one of his friends so eloquently expressed once. This couldn't have been a more perfect description of him.

Coincidentally, it was also hurricane season in Florida and a storm was coming our way. In the midst of this unfortunate circumstance, we were making sure to prepare our home for what was to come. After having spent some time at hospice one day, late into the night we decided we'd go get some rest. We had arrived home, taken our shoes off and all plopped down in the living room. We were silent, emotionless, nearly numb. With not very much else to say, we dispersed to our respective rooms. Angel closed the door behind him. Only thirty minutes had gone by since we'd been home, and then we got the call that he had passed on to be with the Lord. Though we knew it was coming, we were absolutely devastated. The final good-byes were now in order. His mother, aunt, and stepfather were present as people showed up in droves to hold his hand and pay their respects.

Of all people, the last one I'd expect to call and pay their respects in Dee's last moments, and with a barrage of tears and regret, was Angel's father as he told Dee how much he appreciated him for what he had done for Angel. Recognizing for himself that he wasn't the best father to Angel and thanking Dee wholeheartedly for the way he stepped up in his absence. Forever indebted to him, he would say. Words I never thought I'd hear. Dee's passing marked an end at which we didn't want to arrive. Now we'd have to brace ourselves for both the literal and figurative storm to follow.

Grief is an everlasting emotion. Though time passes and our hearts heal, it's a constant pain in your chest you just can't seem to get rid of. We had a lot of repairing to do, which meant grief counseling was necessary for us as a family, more specifically for Angel. He went on to describe him in his eulogy as his "person." I could feel the knot forming in my throat as I tearfully watched him read what he had so carefully put together. He held back the tears, trying to get through this knowing all eyes were on him as he stood at that podium. It's as if he recognized this was his last chance to honor Dee. He took this task on quite confidently. I was sur-prised at just how poised he was as he described his loss. Dee was "the one he could talk to about anything." His right hand, his confidant, his hero. The father-son bond was evident even beyond the grave.

As expected, the calls from my mother continued during this time. She knew we needed her, and she made herself available to us. All the while continuing to set boundaries to allow for my own personal healing. She has a way of turning things around and causing additional anxiety, so it was critical that I make space for her in small increments. Our most real concern subsequently became the literal eye of the storm and the hurricane's effects on us at this time. We had prepared properly and even agreed to withstand the dark stormy nights with Dee's wife, kids, and his family in their home. This, in many ways, seemed to help with healing. At least, for me, it did. Knowing that we were all in one place to look after one another I know also pleased Dee. Being surrounded by the place he called home and his things was also a great source of comfort. The timing couldn't have been any more pre-destined. Leading up to the memorial service and viewing was a difficult time, but we prayed through it. We celebrated his life as he would have wanted, in full National Football League jersey, super bowl party vibe. This helped to make it less of a somber occasion and more of a celebration of life. As you can imagine, yes, my mother was present. Doting over her love for him and saddened by the turn of events that led to here. She showed her appreciation for Dee and his family, as they have always been so welcoming to us. And we would continue to pay it forward.

Chapter 18

PICKING UP THE PIECES

With Dee's passing, so much had changed in our world. It was clear things would never be the same. He had become such an important part of our lives. Though we didn't see each other all the time, he was present in all moments. Angel received daily messages from him; one in the morning, one in the afternoon, and another in the evening. They usually read like this, "Good morning Boog. Have a great day at school!" "Good afternoon Boog, how was school?" "Good night Boog, love you." All messages he'd miss terribly moving forward. I saw the shift in Angel's moods, the change in his stride, and the melancholy manner in which he carried on with his day. He would never be the same. Yet, somehow, through all the grief counseling and biblical readings we did together, he managed to find his way to accept the inevitable. Angel kept items he'd made for Dee since grade school very close to his heart. He was given select clothing items that belonged to Dee, which he would cherish forever. He also managed to dedicate a space for Dee in his bedroom. It was sweet to see, and it warmed my heart to witness the love they shared and what they would continue to share in both this world and beyond.

In those terrible times of grief, it was difficult to see Angel struggle through his emotions. Not long after, he developed a relationship with a young lady that would semi-fill the void he was feeling, but it was clearly just a distraction. Not the best of influences, in my opinion, as she created turmoil in our home. Angel began to do things we didn't approve of, and his temper was escalating when we'd approach him about disagreements. This, my friends, was the start of what would be the most difficult time of his teen life for us. It was absolute torture. I often looked at him like, "Who are you?!" You are not the sweet little child I raised. The logical side of me understood his behavior considering, by this time, he had experienced so much loss. His paternal grandmother, Dee, and, in the years prior, he had lost his very first four-legged love in a tragic car accident. So much to process in such a short period of time—I knew he was struggling.

In the same way, he was experiencing growing pains that we couldn't avoid. It was bound to happen. After over a year in his relationship with this young lady, it ended abruptly. She'd been a cushion for him in that rough time of grieving. A welcomed distraction. Angel, the ultimate gentleman, exceeded the expectations of his romantic partners. He celebrated each special milestone, and yes that included the monthly anniversary dates. His courtship swag was on point.

It was bittersweet to see the downfall. I felt how my mother must have felt with me at that moment. I was there to mend his broken heart. But all the while I knew it was necessary. We got through it, thankfully.

Amid this, Mike and I embarked on our private journey to procreate. We felt there was no better time than now to bring a blessing into this world. This new baby would give us a sense of happiness we hadn't experienced in some time. A new life to bring into this world to receive all the love we were so willing to give. Maybe in some way, for me it was also a welcomed distraction. Coming to terms with the fact that my firstborn was growing up left me with an empty feeling inside. Could it be possible to do it all over again and relieve Angel of my overbearing mommy ways? At least, that was one way to look at it.

After some time trying the good old fashion way, we decided to seek some medical guidance. Not having been able to bring a life into this world naturally due to my own female hormonal complications, we solicited the help of professionals. This meant the in-vitro fertilization (IVF) process would become our new joint venture. We embarked on two IVF sessions in search of our little blessing. Sadly, both failed. What soon followed would be a period of depression unlike any other. Once again, it resurfaced. My feelings of worthlessness and brokenness rushed toward me like a tidal wave. One day, I'll share my IVF journey, but in the meantime, I'd like to say that I hold a special place in my heart for all the women who have tried to conceive but couldn't, who did conceive and lost the pregnancy, and who've had the distinct opportunity to hold a rainbow baby in their arms.

Truth is, part of the reason I was so dedicated to this process, besides the obvious reason of being ready to start a family with Mike, was that I felt I needed help with finding another love that would occupy my mental space. Mothering a "rebellious" teenager for me was the most heart-wrenching experience. And, though our struggles weren't nearly as bad as other families have experienced, the fact that I had given up my entire life, made sacrifices, and ensured to focus on only him made it harder to deal with. I beat myself up quite often about the things that I may have done wrong as a single parent while working on lifting myself up by reminding myself of all the things I did right. They call that mom guilt. And I was certainly guilty.

We involved Angel in our IVF journey. I sometimes think back to this decision to include him and wonder if I did the right thing. In some ways, I believe he too was rooting for us. An only child for so long, I think he was hoping to have a little someone to love that shared my genes too. Luckily, he handled it much better than I did. The tables had turned at the news of our failed attempts and it was he who was comforting me at this time. Flashing back to the difficulties my mother had conceiving, it seemed as though my life was a repeat of hers at this exact moment. It wasn't until my brother was sixteen years old that she was able to conceive my sister and, with some complications, me. So, I started to explore the genetic makeup of the females in our family.

Though there have been plenty of women, both aunts and cousins and my very own sister that birthed three to four children, there were also a handful of women in our family that were only able to birth one. I followed the lineage to my maternal grandfather, for he was the link by which some of us just weren't able to have more than one child. From the top, it was my aunt, Celeste, then my aunt Tati, my cousin Milagros, and me. Not very many of us. I later found that we had a male in the family that had also experienced issues with procreating, though he later was able to conceive via IVF. It was such an interesting thing to explore. Just goes to show your genetic makeup is pivotal to your own life and its unfolding.

I'll never forget that call from the doctor as she communicated the final results. Both Mike and I were on a three-way call, hearing the doctor tell us that it was unsuccessful, then she carried on providing us with options to move forward in trying. Noting that we could consider another round, though this time with more intense hormonal treatment. Something I couldn't even begin to ponder. My heart broke into a million pieces. Not only because of yet another "failure" but also because of everything I had already put my body through in these last months. Yes, it may have been a welcome distraction from all the chaos around me, though, not so much at this cost. Mike was understanding and didn't pressure me to give it another go. Deep down inside, I knew he wanted to, but not at the expense of my own well-being.

Talks with my mother in these moments were tearful. She, again, provided me with much comfort as she understood the struggle of trying to conceive. It was helpful to hear encouragement from her. But I knew it was time to move on. Prior to starting this last IVF cycle, Mike and I made a deal. We would travel in lieu of trying again. It would give me something to look forward to, something positive to expect. Something bright and airy to envision in such a dark time. I was eager to move past this season of our lives.

Shortly after, we began talking about Mike's retirement plans. Having been in the law enforcement field for twenty years, he was ready to make his investments work for him. Being the genius businessman he was, he was always looking into lucrative opportunities. We discussed franchise investments, looking at all of them across the board and discussing many options. Dee's wife happened to start her own franchise, and being new to this franchise world, we thought this would probably be our best bet since we were like "family." Surely she'd have our best interest at heart, right? We'd been through so much and had provided such a support system to them in their darkest hours. Not that she owed us anything, but we felt secure in this way. We crunched the numbers and well, at first glance, it seemed to work out in our favor. We immediately put things in place to make this happen. From establishing our Limited Liability Company (LLC) to liquidating retirement funds, seeking accountants, and attorneys to help us through this process until we signed on the dotted line. This would take on the form of our "new baby." Clearly, travel took a back seat. The chance to create a legacy for our family and find financial freedom became a priority. Seeing as how we were now in the hole for this huge IVF bill that reaped no real results. We were ready to challenge ourselves.

We gathered a group of our closest friends and family to witness the honor of opening our new establishment. We were proud of this new journey we were about to embark on. Our loved ones knew that this was a major move for us. Reflecting on the years Mike had invested serving the community, nearly risking his life, earning every penny which we spent paying for each and every item in this place made me all the more emotional. To see his hard work and dedication in the form of a new investment and see how we collectively worked to make this happen was truly heartwarming. We dotted all the *i*s and crossed all the *t*s, ensuring we were covering all bases; showing my mother that I was walking in her footsteps meant a lot to me as well. Moreover, having her present to witness what Mike and I were building together was the icing on the cake. Yet, when I think back to this moment, I don't quite recall her jumping for joy. I felt she was present that evening, seemingly more so out of a sense of responsibility. She was accompanied by my older sister, but as soon as we wrapped up the grand opening celebration, she retreated to my sister's home. The true reward for me was the opportunity to fellowship with my family over dinner, considering the grand opening was all work and show. Networking, if you will. So you can understand how her decision to skip the dinner hurt my feelings. For me, it was just another example of a moment she didn't fully experience with me. I wanted more, but all I could do was settle. After all, what choice did I really have in the matter? I wondered if I was overreacting.

Though I grew up watching one of the most successful women in the beauty industry (in my eyes), my mother's experience as a beauty professional wouldn't prepare me for this journey. This particular beauty specialty was one that required a lot of training in a competitive market. Aesthetic salons were opening up left and right, offering the best and newest techniques. Considering Mike's background and mine were in the Justice system, we felt a bit out of place, but we were confident in the Franchisor's promises that we would be guided every step of the way. We believed it. Weeks turned into months, months turned into a year, and I was steadfast, focused on doing everything I possibly could to ensure the business's success, as was he. For a self-described introvert like myself, pushing myself out of my comfort zone was critical. Our finances depended on it. Determined not to fail, we pushed forward. Still maintaining my full-time employment, I was sure that we could get through this. Dedicated to my work, and yet I spent my nights and weekends working overtime to make up for the lack of presence in the establishment.

Yes, this made it all the more challenging, but it was my saving grace in the long run. Even when the unfavorable side of the industry reared its ugly head, I held my head high. When the cattiness, pettiness, and unprofessionalism started to display itself, I maintained laser focus. By now, I was realizing we were alone in this battle. It was every man for himself. Ulterior motives unseen, we were ignorant of the fact that those who smiled in our faces were really plotting behind our backs. Or at least that's how we saw it. Until flight or fight mode kicked in.

The following two years were a blur. We expected to put in work and have sleepless nights. Expense after expense. Staff issues. We understood them all. What we didn't expect was to be let down by those we trusted the most. *This* was one of the most eye-opening encounters of our lives. Over two hundred thousand dollars down the figurative drain. The business was successfully holding rank against the competition. Yet somehow we felt we were continuing to spin our wheels. There was no consideration from anyone we had invested in, with the exception of minimal help here and there, we were spent, no pun intended.

Some months were exceptional profit-wise, while in others we were deep in the whole. In an effort to maximize our investment, we started to get creative. Incorporating new services and getting certified to provide those services so that Mike and I would be able to balance out the costs. Yet, we were still getting the short end of the stick. A large part of it was the discrepancies within the franchise. The lack of forethought toward the new location owners. Until one day we just couldn't do it any longer. We began to look for options to sell the business. Reaching out to franchise attorneys for legal advice on what would be the best way to go about this, to release us of what had unfortunately become a blood-sucking endeavor.

I'll be honest, it wasn't easy to come to terms with the fact that a good chunk of our retirement money was dwindling away. But it was Mike who assured me that our peace of mind was worth much more than our egos. Words I'd be grateful for for months to come. It's as if a burden was lifted off our shoulders the day we decided to let it go. But not before a huge part of me had felt like a failure. I continued to find ways to reassure myself that this was the best thing to do, to resign our roles as franchise owners and find our way back to living again.

But before our new life began, we'd first have to officially close the horrid business chapter that preceded us. It just so happened that as we neared finalizing the termination of our contractual agreement, our world was about to experience its first worldwide pandemic. While we were literally in discussions about the exchange of our franchise, worried about how this would affect the few faithful staff we had, and trying to accommodate our contractual obligations, we were now forced to temporarily close our doors because of the coronavirus pandemic. The novel human coronavirus disease, COVID-19, had become the fifth documented pandemic since the 1918 pandemic flu.[8]

We didn't know to what extent this turn of events in our nation would affect our business, but what we did know is that we were relieved to be on our way out. We still had obligations to meet and loose ends to tie up, so we were responsible business owners until we were no longer able to provide. We were depleted mentally, physically, and emotionally and now we had a new challenge to contend with: establishing Health Guidelines for the sake of our staff as a precaution and ensuring our clients they were safe. Ultimately, the shutdown within the beauty industry was lifted shortly before we were to officially turn in our keys. We walked out of that establishment heads held high, vowing to put an end to an enlightening stage of our lives. For, in all honesty, monetary gains would never amount to the spiritual gains we would have thereafter.

Chapter 19

PEACE OF MIND, PIECE OF CAKE

S o it was time to recalibrate. I joined the club of many who found the quarantine to be a *Godsend*. It's like the Lord knew we needed to slow down. To breathe. To refocus and turn our attention to what mattered most: our family, our health, and our lives. Self couldn't have been more important during this period. In fact, I believe I trained my whole life for this. As an introvert, isolation was my safe place. My safe haven. For in that moment of stillness, I discovered myself. I was most comfortable here. Both Mike and I were blessed to have still been employed in the field of public service where we would be considered essential workers. So for us, work didn't entirely stop.

But in this period, watching the news became depressing. The dark and gloomy images forever etched in my mind. The sullen and exhausted faces of men, women, and children were heartbreaking. The daily reports of closed businesses, lost jobs, and bankruptcies as was our most recent franchise experience. A world with which we were very much familiar. The thought of not knowing when this would end left many families feeling hopeless. Without a backup plan, many were left to find creative ways to maintain and feed their families. Food banks, community food drives, and other community resources were tapped into and as a result, also tapped out. Cohabiting became the new norm. Necessity called it to be so. Families cramming into the only household arrangement they could afford also led to a spike in hardship both emotionally, mentally, and physically. Businesses suffered greatly during the pandemic, and years later, they continue to struggle. The US Government provided some assistance in this nationwide state of emergency by way of stimulus funds and unemployment benefits, but these didn't last very long for those who were suffering the loss of a job, their home, or loved ones. Every day, I felt more and more blessed.

My mother was in a state of panic, as were most in the country and around the world in the face of global uncertainty. She was locked onto the television watching the number of deaths rise day in and day out. Suffering from high blood pressure, this was not at all recommended as the stress would only cause additional complications. Needless to say, this was a concern for her. All the years of stressing and worrying were catching up to her and here we were now experiencing something that was unheard of in our lifetime. Something that didn't seem to have an end. Something that didn't discriminate between the young and the old, the healthy and the unhealthy, nor within any race and ethnicity. It was an invisible equal opportunity killer. This is what made it the scariest. Conversations with her were nerve-racking. So, I built a safe cocoon in my space, blocking out all possible negative energy.

During this time, I buried my head in the Bible. The Word was my saving grace. Time in meditation became my solace, and the peace I experienced within the confines of my home was extraordinary. I was finally able to get back to *me*. I wasn't going to allow anything or anyone to create noise in my world. As you can imagine, I was not the best person for my mother to talk with, seeing as we just weren't speaking the same language. She was on edge, and I was in Zen. So our conversations went kind of like this. Loosely translated from Spanish of course:

> **Mom:** Goodness! Have you heard how many people have died?
> **Me:** No Ma. Luckily I've stopped watching the news. It's gotten way too depressing.
> **Mom:** But you need to watch it; how else are you going to know what's going on?
> **Me:** I get all relevant local information regarding the state of our pandemic and any emergency management needs and responses from my job so, I don't watch the news to avoid panic.
> **Mom:** Well, I will continue to watch the news because I need to know what's going on.

She moved on and called my sister and brother, talking with them more in-depth about her fears and sharing all the day's news, reporting several times a day. Instilling panic in them that they would then pass down to those around them often leading to arguments and a mix of emotions. This . . . this is the very thing I wanted to avoid. There comes a time in our lives when we must be selective. Choosing what we dedicate time and energy to is critical to our own well-being. Suddenly, we find that the things that used to matter, especially in these times, just don't matter anymore. All of a sudden, the rising numbers of virus cases and deaths make us realize that tomorrow is not promised, and we must learn to live our best lives today.

This time alone led me to re-discover who I was at the core. It took some isolation, prayer, meditation, motivational podcasts, book readings, conversations with my husband, my friends, and even strangers, as well as some deep soul-searching to realize that, at the end of the day, the one person I must be happy with is me. I can only control myself, my thoughts, my reactions, and my own happiness. I have a choice now to reframe my thinking and, in turn, reframe my life.

There was a little voice in my head over the past fifteen years that kept calling me to serve. Serving the community is what I did, and still do. But this call to serve was different. I had to serve those people that I couldn't see or touch. I had to reach the masses. This call to serve meant I had to, once again, push myself outside of my comfort zone. That same little voice in my head reminded me that writing is my passion. So what was I waiting for? Why didn't I fully commit to this dream? Everywhere I turned, during my rediscovery, I was led in the same direction. Whether it was a comment from someone or a sign at a certain time of the day that confirmed it was time to sit with my thoughts and get it all down on paper. For years, I'd like to say I felt confident. I felt I believed in myself "enough." I felt I was doing just as I should have been doing, given my current circumstances. I was accomplished. In the eyes of the world, at least, I'd be considered "accomplished." So here's the recap:

I purchased my first home, on my own, as a single mother by the age of thirty-two. I earned my Bachelor's Degree in Criminal Justice at the age of twenty-two and my Master's Degree in Public Administration at the age of thirty-one; I had held a career for over thirteen years with county government and, prior to that, held a position with the Federal Government while in college. As you have read, while living at home, I helped provide for my family, and when I moved I'd send money home to my mother to help her pay her bills, as is the custom in our culture. You always take care of your home, even while juggling taking care of your own. Later on, along with my hardworking husband, I invested in stocks and IRAs. We set ourselves up for retirement or for the right investment opportunity . . . whichever came first. And we did just that, took a big chunk of those funds and invested in a business. We had accomplished that much. So, needless to say, I thought I believed in myself enough.

Fast forward to a less-than-fruitful business investment, the crushing of our spirits, and the disappointment in ourselves. We were broken. I didn't understand the power of intentionality and thinking positive thoughts until this very moment. In our upbringing, to some extent, we have been bred to believe in spirituality. Whether it's Christianity, Hinduism, Buddhism, Catholicism—you name it—the focus was always to believe in a power greater than oneself. Wherein we sought in those times of difficulty, that very power that would pull us out from the depths of despair. Praying to that mighty power for strength and understanding. That's what we did. We prayed and prayed, and prayed.

Certainly, delving back into that spiritual place was comforting, as always. But I felt I needed wisdom and better understanding. I needed more to help me put the pieces of my shattered spirit together. I read up on Buddhist practices—on his holiness, the Dalai Lama, the practices of sage burning, and on crystals provided by Mother Nature and their meanings. On becoming one with the very things that the Lord has blessed us with . . . the beauty of nature and our surroundings. This aromatherapy, and digging into natural-based practices, is what led me to create the ability to *believe* that, *in me*, there was *great power*. Not that I didn't "somewhat" already know that. I simply didn't know it to this extent.

The more knowledge and understanding I developed, the more in tune with myself I became. The more I started to see the signs and hear His voice. The more I was nudged in the direction of the things I've kept pushing aside all my life. My love for reading, my love for writing, my need to escape into the wonders of the outside world—all of it increasing. And so I found solace in traveling alone. If somehow my day took me near the beach, I'd make it a point to visit the beach and bury my toes in the sand, transfixed by the rolling of the waves in awe of His works. To focus on even the smallest things like the shrubbery growing out of the beach dunes or the birds soaring in the sky. I intentionally sought quiet, creative earthly places. Visiting local gardens, reveling in the masterpiece of all that He has created. Finding all the surrounding goodness, even during a bike ride, or a walk around the block. I noticed a red robin that kept appearing each day at the same time, as if to catch my attention, leading me to create a refuge for them, where I could marvel at their majesty each day, so I got a bird feeder. I became more in tune with my surroundings. Focusing inward and vowing to remove myself slowly from all outside distractions. This awakened me. This was true enlightenment.

I started to visualize that which I did not previously see. My knowledge continued to multiply as I came to understand my purpose. My true purpose. See, with my current position in the community, I already knew that my calling/purpose was to serve. But it wasn't until I was in this enlightened state of mind that I realized serving, for me, was going to multiply in a myriad of ways, with the use of my talents, my skills, and my resources. In this walk, I met many people, people I know were divinely placed. Yet another confirmation that I was on the right track. Just the thought of it made my heart skip a beat (thank you, Lord). So I continued to pour all my attention into those exact things that were guiding my path. I learned that I needed to set my intentions, affirm what I want, and, in turn, it will all manifest. So I did that by creating vision boards. Seeing those very things on the board come to fruition brought me life. I'm on track! I created specific goals for myself, then looked back at those goals to see what I had accomplished.

YES! Another win. I removed negativity from my life. *This raised my frequency and allowed me to rise to the highest version of myself* (as learned from the great Jen Sincero, in *You Are a Badass*; Running Press Book Publishers, 2017).

All it took was some reprogramming of my brain, the need to overpower deeply rooted beliefs that even I was oblivious to. Wow! What spending time with yourself will do. I created a daily spiritual practice to develop the keen discipline I now knew I was going to need on this journey. I learned *we don't need more; we just need to do more with what we know.* That *daily intention setting made my day more meaningful and reminded me that I, at the very least, should not harm others.* I also learned that *once I set new intentions,* I needed to hold myself accountable, and go back and *re-evaluate old ones.* (From the *Book of Joy*, By H. H., the Dalai Lama, and Archbishop Desmond Tutu; Avery, 2016).

I asked myself these questions:

How do you want to feel?
What things would you like to experience?
What personal qualities/strengths do you want to develop?

I then created affirmations to accompany those thoughts Like: "I feel . . ." or "I have . . ." affirmations that pulled me into a connection with the positive things I wanted to see reflected in my life. For instance, I feel happy, healthy, whole, confident, positive, blessed, worthy, etc. Even if you don't 100 percent feel those things. Put it out there that you do, and, believe me, you will. I have opportunities flowing in abundance; I have the means to bless others; I have an amazing support system, etc. This puts you in the position to create opportunities for those things you want to have in your life. You can even get very specific with this. In fact, I've learned, that the more specific you are . . . the better! I have a million-dollar writing deal. I have a house on the hill in Ireland. The same can be done with I am. I am wealthy. I am gifted. I am talented. Have fun with it. This is your chance to dream.

> The potential of your power is determined by the strength of your power source.

Read that again: *the potential of your power is determined by the strength of your power source.* What are you giving power to in your day-to-day? Whenever I had a bad day, I'd repeat this *mantra: He loves me and is for me, this fills me with joy and confidence.* This redirected my thinking, bringing me back from what could have been a dark place. I vividly remember being asked by a friend, as I counseled her through a difficult time, "How do you remain so positive?" Well, this is it. Redirecting my thinking. Remembering **Whose I am**, and what **He** has for me.

Re-evaluate all the things you think you are not. Open the door of opportunity to become all that you want and are des-tined to be. The Word says so in **Romans 12:2**, "Do not be conformed to this world, but be transformed by the renewal of your mind, that by testing you may discern what is the will of God, what is good, and acceptable, and perfect." Can you say, *powerful*?! He led me right to that.

And each day I saw my attitude change, my dreams grow more vivid, my attitude get bolder, and my spirit more joyful.

Today, I'm finally living out the life I was destined to live; it's one in which I'm not at all concerned about the opinions of others, or the stares and the judgments. I am living my life, just as He designed it to be . . . purposeful. After all, as best explained by the greats Ralph Waldo Emerson and Eleanor Roosevelt herself,

"The **purpose** of **life** is not to be happy. It is to be useful, to be honorable, to be compassionate, to have it make some difference that you have lived and lived well."

". . . To **live** it, to taste experience to the utmost, to reach out eagerly and without fear of a newer and richer experience."

Chapter 20

LIGHT AT THE END OF THE TUNNEL

L ife throws us many curve balls along our journey. You could be in a total state of enlightenment and *BOOM*, here comes a boulder careening down the steep mountain and coming your way. How do you find the motivation to keep going?

It's hard to describe but stay with me . . . I'll try. Have you ever been to your local fair, carnival, or amusement park? Ever gotten on that UFO ride? The one that spins and spins and spins so much it adheres you to the walls? And now, you can't move. You're stuck. Then the ride starts to slow down. As it slows, you feel your limbs, little by little. You can move your face now, your fingers, your arms, then your legs, and your toes. By the time it comes to a complete stop, you have a sense of stillness. You may be dizzy, but you've got this serene sense about you. In this moment, you have to get the rest of the earth to fall in line with where *you* are. Your legs feel like Jell-O, and you feel like Bambi, learning to walk again. That, ladies and gents, is what it feels like to be enlightened. The UFO ride is the world trying to keep us from our greatness. All the things that trip us up; our fears: our insecurities, our past, our families, our kids, and fake friends. The list goes on and on; the list of all the things that jump in our paths looking to bulldoze over everything we've worked so hard to build.

Here's the good news though, after I've been on that horrific ride called life's trip-ups, now I have a variety of skills with which I've armed myself. Meditation, intention setting, affirming, and manifesting will ricochet those things right off me. Like a superpower. It's like wearing some blingin' impenetrable armor (appeasing my sci-fi fans out there). However, just beware, your mind will play tricks on you. At any point, you could go back to your self-defeating way of thinking. If you're focused, it will only be for a brief second. If you're struggling, this may take a day or two, at most a week. But you will bounce right back. In reality, *you're indestructible. You're able to withstand any pressure, pain, or weight that comes your way.* It may not feel like that in the thick of it but think about it. No, *seriously* . . . think about all the things you've been through. The very things you didn't think you'd ever be able to get over. That first heartbreak, the lost job, the failed test, the car accident, the house fire…you name it, it was horrible. You didn't see a way out. But *you did* make it out! You made it through. You're here, *now*, reading this. Won't *He* do it?!? Just like that.

Unfortunately, we beat ourselves up way too much. We think one failure is going to jeopardize our entire plan. What we didn't know was *that moment was destined to be*. You ask, "How can something 'bad for me' actually be meant to be?" Well, have you ever considered looking at things from this perspective? Let's say, (real-life example here people), you've planned your entire day. You've made a list. A to-do list with a host of things you've got to accomplish today. This list is in chronological order from highest to lowest priority. You're two items into the list when someone throws a monkey wrench into your plans. What do you do? Initially, you get frustrated. You start a mental rundown of that list. You get even more frustrated now. You start playing Tetris with these items in your head. Can you still catch up? And guess what . . . you drive yourself crazy. Now, you've got an attitude and you're frustrated. That whole moment stole your joy. But why? Instead of thinking in reverse, think in fast-forward. What things could this "inconvenience" just have removed from your path? Slow down. What do you actually have time to do **now** that you *didn't* put on your list? Breathe. Think. Pray. Turn up the music. Reduce the velocity. Do you realize how seeing through rose-colored glasses gives you a new perspective?

You've heard this one before, "Life is 10 percent what happens to you and 90 percent how you react to it." Words spoken by one of the most revered evangelical Christian Pastors of our time, Mr. Charles R. Swindoll.

In her writing, "Why Limiting Beliefs Hold You Back in Life and What to Do About It," Liz Huber notes that *the sum of our beliefs, both positive ones and negative ones make up our mindset and thus our idea of reality.*[9]

It literally changes your view of almost everything in life. It can also be a reflection of our strongest beliefs. Sometimes our thoughts are shaped by what we think of ourselves—what we think we are or what we think we are not capable of accomplishing. Most of the time, we force ourselves into this tiny little box. We're accustomed to thinking that everything we do must be done inside this six-by-six-foot frame, so we suffocate ourselves. Why not consider stepping outside the box? Breaking it down, laying it flat, rolling around on it, then sitting back and looking up at the sky. Yes, now you're exposed, but guess what? Now you've got more room. To think, to breathe, to stretch. Yes, it's just that easy. It's different, but doable.

Michelle Obama said it best in her book, *Becoming* (Crown Viking Press, 2018), "Move in forward motion, evolving and reaching continuous progress toward a better self."

Never let yourself stay immobile for too long, always look for growth. In each moment, look for opportunities to improve your own being. You were not meant to be stagnant. You were meant to grow. So push yourself, even when it's uncomfortable. In fact, especially when it's uncomfortable because that is the environment in which growth thrives. Rumi said, "Very little grows on jagged rock. Be ground. Be crumbled, so wildflowers will come up where you are." Evaluate your mindset. Consider all the things that could go right in your day. Then consider all the things that could go wrong. Are you equipped to handle it? If you are, kudos to you, grasshopper. You're well on your way. If you're not, hun . . . we've got some work to do.

Be *fearless* in the pursuit of what sets your soul on *fire*.

What sets my soul on fire? For me, it's serving people. I know that now. Like, I really, really, 100 percent, positively know that this is my purpose. And I mean serving others in many ways, whether it's with my volunteerism, speaking engagements, within my career, as a mentor, in my community, personally… or to my friends and family. My passion is serving others.

For years, I was tripped up about my purpose. I got to a point in my life where I'd actually asked myself that question. What's my purpose? Am I living out my life as I should? Am I doing too much or doing too little? Is there more I can do with the talents I have? Should I be less focused on people, and more focused on myself or my family? All of these were burning questions that in many ways kept ringing in my head. I don't know if any of you recall the big discussion that was spiked on this topic with the release of the book, *A Purpose Driven Life,* by Pastor Rick Warren (Zondervan 2002). It was the question of the century. How do we find our purpose? Seems more people were asking themselves this question at that time than at any other time in history. It was transformational. So much so, Oprah Winfrey did a full special on this book. She interviewed the author, and just like that . . . the entire world was turned onto the readings. Was it a practice? A belief system? Not sure, as much as I keep telling myself to read this book, I still haven't gotten around to it. I believe I've read similar books that probably express parallel sentiments, but it is definitely on my *must-read* list. Though I digress, the point is . . . it was no different for me. I had to *narrow it down*, or did I? What was my purpose?

I sought to find it. I'm an observant person by nature. Within my surroundings and even more so within myself. I do a lot of evaluating of the SELF. My own behaviors, my reactions, and my thought process. I think it's important to do this so that we understand who we are. If you don't know **yourself**, then how do you expect others to know? So, in this soul search, I kept getting nudged in the same direction. There are several things I've always been pulled toward; my love of reading and writing, and my love of people. It took a lot for me to even agree that I *loved* people because—my husband would laugh at this, but—for a time, I used to say the exact opposite because of disappointments in dealing with others. So in my personal life, I pretty much kept to myself, maintaining a safe distance from those I considered to have "shaky" personalities. I was, and still am to an extent, really private for that reason.

In my professional life, however? I dove right into serving. I volunteered in the community, helped develop mentorship programs, accepted opportunities to speak and encourage others, as well as taking on a lead role to advocate in general. I'm an advocate by nature. There are a number of different causes that are near and dear to my heart, but in general, it's the realness of just helping people through tough times that draws me. The ability to help someone see outside of their dark moments. For those that are simply struggling with transitions in life and need some guidance. I like to see the growth in people. I'd say it may be attributed to seeing and feeling the growth within *myself.* Such an amazing feeling—I want others to experience it as well.

Along with serving and writing, I've always been intrigued by the human mind: the way it works, the way we think. I remember the episode like it was yesterday, in 1990 on the *Oprah Winfrey Show,* where she interviewed a woman with ninety-two personalities. This woman suffered from dissociative identity disorder caused by years of sexual abuse, which began at the age of two. I was fascinated by the way this woman, with such ease in the transition, would go from answering as one personality, then another. The personalities themselves talk to each other. It's as if she was only a shell of a body that housed these voices, these different people that lived inside of her. 'How was this possible?' I thought. And even more importantly, I felt a sense of deep sadness for her. An ironic connection to such a lonely existence.

It's the one time I recall in my childhood when I combined my genuine compassion for others and writing. I went on to do a writing project in school on the topic of Multiple Personality Disorders. I was nine years old guys, NINE. In fact, I was so moved by the issue I still have the report to this day. No exaggeration there. I'm certain I can go into my closet and find it right now, or somewhere in my garage. The point is, I remember submitting it and thinking, 'I wonder if my teacher is going to think I'm weird for picking this topic to write about?' But I didn't care. It was an issue that concerned me. Naturally, I got an A on this report, but I realized even then that there are so many people with serious traumas who are hurting. They struggle, and I just want to find a way to help, whether it's with my writing, my counsel, my presence, my encouragement, or my inspiration. I just want to help.

My passion: **helping others.** "How do you do it? How did you get here?" I'm asked that more often than you know. Like they say, "If I had a nickel for every time . . ." And my response always is, "But by the Grace of God." I know it's Him. I'm also a major India Arie fan. Some years back I discovered this song of hers, "Thy Will be Done." (Soulbird Music, released 2013) It's been the soundtrack to my life ever since.

So all that to say . . . that sometimes, just sometimes . . . we have signs from very early on in childhood. The things we've been drawn to, the things we like, the things we don't like, the things that bring us joy, the things that make us extremely uncomfortable, the opportunities that present themselves, the jobs we've lost even. All these things and more, combined into one big pile, represent that which you've been guided toward. Mind you, I'm well aware of how life works. We have dreams, desires, and ambitions we seek or would like to seek. Life gets in the way. We have obstacles. We have other things that become "priority" over our dreams, desires, and ambitions. But we keep getting that tap on the shoulder—that opportunity that comes out of nowhere. The person whom you barely know who sends you a message, an article, or a flier (this happened to me) nudging you in the direction of your dreams. All those little signs. *Pay attention!* And go for it. That's how you know. Those are the things that fuel your passion. It sets your soul on fire. Instinctually, your destiny is already awaiting you. It's the push and pull you can't escape. Surrender to the *push*, and you'll see just how far the *pull* will take you.

Chapter 21

FULL CIRCLE

Recall some chapters before, how I expressed that perfection was what I've always strived for? Yeah, well . . . *Fail* is that figurative four-letter-word. You know, like a bad word. Much like the other four-letter F word our parents told us never to say. In the same way, *failing* was the one thing I've avoided all my life. By now you know, I've been a *straight-A student* for as long as I've been a student. Average has never been my thing. I wanted nothing more than to bring a smile to my mother's face when she saw my report card. Granted, half the time she didn't know what she was looking at, what she was reading, or what the grades meant but I was the eager kid who brought the report card home and explained it to her (English to Spanish elementary translation).

As if you haven't noticed by now, I did my best at everything I attempted. When I took on reading, I wanted to be the best reader. When I took on writing, I wanted to be the best writer. When I took on basketball, I wanted to be the only girl on the court that could stand a chance against the boys. I loved the challenge. I loved pushing myself outside the limits. I wanted to be the exception to the rule, always. I loved the thrill of accomplishing something new and crushing it. So, needless to say, when I gave it my all, last place was not what I was shooting for. But failure is also the very thing that held me back from taking risks into adulthood. All of a sudden, that impulsive desire to be the greatest at all costs actually came at a cost. The irony! Becoming an adult brings its own perspective. Suddenly, "failing" at something doesn't only affect you; it also affects those who depend on you, those who have a vested interest in your every move.

In life, I've evidently failed at several things. I "failed" at being perfect, I "failed" in business, I "failed" as a dreamer; remember, there was a point I thought I was failing as a parent (any parent of a teenager has been there before, I know I'm not alone here). The thought of not knowing what was on the other end of that risk was scary, so I avoided it by any means necessary. It took me marrying a risk-taker to be pushed well outside that comfort zone. He showed me how to challenge myself as an adult in ways I didn't think possible. But it took a while. We're both alpha personalities, yet we both have different approaches to success. His was (excuse the term) balls to the wall, go hard or go home. My strategy? I need a Plan A, a Plan B, a Plan C, and a D just in case things go awry.

My very first attempt at releasing that control was investing our life savings in a business that ultimately reaped no *real* rewards. At the end of that experience, I was crushed, as you can imagine. It was exactly the situation I was trying to avoid. But I was reminded of something I kept hearing time and time again before we took that investment plunge. It was the voice of Steve Harvey that echoed in my ears; "The most successful people in this world recognize that taking chances to get what they want is much more productive than sitting around being too scared to take a shot." Every successful person has a story of defeat. If they're lucky, two, or three, or more. With more defeats comes more experiences and learning lessons that lead to success. Though that was difficult to come to terms with at first, everything I dealt with after that major shift was leading me to the same understanding. I dove right into my comfort zone. The Word, and my love of reading.

> *"Everything you do on your journey*
> *contributes to where you're going."*
> —Jen Sincero, *You Are a Badass*

There were so many gems in Jen Sincero's book, but this quote, in particular, inspired me the most. Believing in what was not yet seen, I leaped into manifesting a new life for myself. I found peace of mind and gratitude even in my supposed failures. I loved myself enough to stand in my truth and, in turn, attract the things, people, and opportunities that were aligned with who I truly am. And you can do the same for yourself. In her book, Jen goes on to say, "However easy or rough the growth process toward success—you must be willing to fall down, get up, look stupid, cry, laugh, make a mess, clean it up, and not stop until you get there." *I felt that!*

In the end, we must learn to release those things we hold on to so tightly. We need to create space for all the blessings that have yet to come. Those things were karmically delivered in ways and through people we have never even expected. Open yourself up to the possibilities beyond the so-called "failures." The best is yet to come!

With overcoming failure, we often lose sight of *forgiveness*. Forgiveness of self and others. This is a rough one with which I have struggled a lot. And just when I think I have life under control, here comes another test in dealing with people. I'm sure I'm not alone. So many of us believe that forgiveness means accepting someone's apology and moving past the hurt only to let people back into your life. *Nope! Big n-o!* Forgiveness often looks like "I forgive you because I don't want to carry that heavy burden, but I don't necessarily need you in my space."

I sought counsel from the best advocate I knew regarding this topic. I read deep into the Word of God. For who knows best about forgiveness than He who died for our sins and still chooses to stand tall for us each day? The only way I can "forgive" and move on from those who have hurt me is by entrusting my soul to the only one who sees fit to see me through it. I even pulled out a devotional for this one guy. For seven days, I sat in the understanding of forgiveness. I let Him impart to me the wisdom and knowledge that is necessary to process forgiving someone for the hurt they've caused. There are so many areas of my life I have needed to forgive others for wrongs done to me. I've also had to ask for forgiveness. The Gospel artist Jonathan McReynolds so eloquently expresses it in his song, "People" (EP Moving On, released 2020 by eOne). Go take a listen.

I've sat in silence. I've processed. I've meditated. I've listened. What I've learned about the topic of *forgiveness*:

Forgiveness lets people off the hook.

Refusing to forgive keeps you tied to that person, and who wants that?

They have nothing with which to repay their debt, so release them.

Work through it, name it, express your feelings about it, then let it go.

Resistance wants us to stay in the past. The past is no place for us.

A life of judgment and unforgiveness is a prison. Release yourselves from that prison.

We find ourselves focused on another person's failures rather than on the good we have in life.

Focus on your spiritual lives and joyful relationships. You'll find so much pleasure in this.

Failure to forgive brings resentment and emptiness. This is a horrible emotion to carry around.

Let it go and increase your quality of life.

Genesis 50:20 reads, "You intended to harm me, but God intended it all for good. He brought me to this position so I could save the lives of many people." What an empowering scripture! Now this breathes new life in a moment of brokenness, doesn't it?

Our natural tendency is to treat others the way they treat us. Have you heard the Biblical story of Moses? Oh, he's only one of the most well-known characters in the Bible. See, in Moses, of all the roles he played throughout his life, we're reminded that he was a normal person just like us. For this reason, we relate to him so much. In the times of old, when the Israelites were a threat, Moses being born into the world as an Israelite boy was to be assassinated. His mother, however, felt he was special. So she hid him as long as she could then set him off in the Nile River in a makeshift boat. Rescued by Pharoah's daughter, he was then given back to his mother to nurse. A full circle moment for this tike. In the years that followed, he was raised as royalty. He experienced some hardships, as many of us do, and did some things he was less than proud of. But having always been close with God and redeeming himself as a courageous leader, he would ultimately find his way to his rightful place. Where he belonged, exactly where the Lord placed him.

What if we did like Moses? He asked God for compassion on the hurts of those who hadn't treated him well. This way of thinking will lead you to a life of love, grace, freedom, and forgiveness. And as if to continue with our running theme, yes, forgiveness takes *courage*. May your unending prayer be that God removes from you all bitterness and hatred and replaces it with His perfect love. As long as you refuse to forgive, you continue to give power to that person who did you wrong. Take that power back and gain a life in the process. Let Him be the judge. **First Kings 8:39** says, "Give your people what their actions deserve for you alone know their human heart."

Hurt people, hurt people. And this statement alone is an understanding that… we are not qualified to cast judgment on others when we don't know what internal struggle they face. We also aren't mighty enough to hold this ability.

Live from a place of growth instead of brokenness. The Word says, "We should no longer think of anyone as impure or unclean" (**Acts 10:28**).

What I've learned, having had to do my own forgiving in life, is that true forgiveness isn't so much because the other person deserves it. Rather, because you deserve peace. You learn that holding on to the grudge, the anger, and the resentment takes so much energy. That same energy can be used toward good. Holding onto these negative emotions can lead to sickness. The stress that comes from it, though you claim to be "unbothered," starts to take a toll on you both emotionally and physically. Before you know it, your attitude begins to change. The way you treat others begins to change and is reflected in the way you carry yourself. It's like a nagging pain in your side. A heavy weight on your shoulders. It never goes away. The only way to release such a burden is to genuinely **forgive and set boundaries**—in whatever way that looks like for you.

"Instead, be kind to each other, tenderhearted, forgiving one another just as God through Christ has forgiven you" **Ephesians 4:32**. For what better way can we come to terms with forgiveness than through the Word of God? I don't know about you, but this alone brings me peace and comfort.

So today I look at myself in the mirror and I realize just how alike we all are. We've all had triumphs and trials we've had to overcome—some greater than others. It's important that we learn to forgive ourselves. For the times we thought we were less than. The times we thought we were not worthy of love. That we didn't meet the mark, or that we were unloving. Learn to forgive yourself. But, most importantly, forgive those who have knowingly or unknowingly hurt you. For all the things that broke your spirit. For all the things that hurt your feelings. For the actions and inactions of those you love who were, in turn, unable to reciprocate that love. If there's one vital thing I've learned, it is that people can only do the best they can with what they know how and with what they have. Be willing to walk away and create a safe distance when these people trouble your spirit.

Pray for healing for them and for yourself. It may be difficult to see our loved ones go through life not being able to fully experience God's glory. One thing we know for sure is it's not our responsibility. We are merely responsible for our own happiness. Yet we say, "If we could only impart all the knowledge we've learned over the years and plant it in their brains, maybe then they'll see life differently. Maybe then they'd remember just how lovely it is to live life in bold pursuit of happiness." To think that it may take some kind of catastrophe to happen to soften us up and bring us back to reality. 'Tis the circle of life. It's the fate we've had since Genesis. From the beginning of time, we've seen good come from bad. Eventually, it will come back around. All we can do is impart the bit of wisdom we know to those who will accept it. And to those who follow in our footsteps—our children, the future generation—may we leave them a world that is worthy of living.

ACKNOWLEDGMENTS

W ell, it's official. *The book has been written.* I still can't believe I'm saying that. Writing this was more difficult than I had imagined. Not because I didn't think I was skilled enough, but because I knew it meant I had to be vulnerable. Although this period of my life was filled with many ups and downs, none of it would have been possible without the investment of the following individuals:

First and foremost, to my mother. Without you, there would be no me. Though we've faced difficult circumstances over the years, as a mother myself, I can now see that you were only doing the best you could with that which you were equipped. Nonetheless, I'd say you were successful in your parenting. As I sit here typing this, I acknowledge how the morals, values, and ethics you shared led me to this very moment. I pray we continue to grow together, and that you are able to live your life unapologetically and joyously for the rest of your days.

(Spanish Translation) *En primer lugar, a mi madre. Sin ti no existiría yo. Aunque hemos enfrentado circunstancias difíciles a lo largo de los años, como madre, ahora puedo ver que solo estabas haciendo lo mejor que podías con lo que estabas equipada. No obstante, diría que tuviste éxito en tu crianza. Mientras me siento aquí escribiendo esto, reconozco cómo la moral, los valores y la ética que compartio me llevaron a este mismo momento. Ruego que sigamos creciendo juntas y que puedas vivir tu vida sin disculpas y con alegría el resto de tus días.*

To my father, though blood does not connect us, you are truly that . . . *my father.* Your role in my life was essential to understanding and feeling that earthly fatherly love. I've learned many things from your powerful demeanor, and I will carry them on for the rest of my days. Thank you for stepping up to the plate.

(Spanish Translation) *A mi padre. Aunque la sangre no nos une, eres verdaderamente eso... MI PADRE. Su papel en mi vida fue fundamental para comprender y sentir ese amor de padre terrenal. He aprendido muchas cosas de su comportamiento poderoso, y las llevaré el resto de mis días. Gracias por dar un paso al frente.*

To my sponsor, thank you for your donation. Truth is, I'm made up of two people, and that I can't deny. My gratitude comes in the form of this acknowledgment.

To my son, where do I begin? This book was birthed because of you. You made me want to be better, do better, love better, and provide you with more than I could have ever envisioned. Thank you for your support. For the nights I needed some feedback. For your candid responses in relation to our life story, which I share. For the inspiration you are for me today and since God blessed me to carry you into this world. I am beyond honored to be your mother. Can't wait to see all the extraordinary things life has in store for you.

To my husband. For your advice, helping me stay focused by creating a daily schedule, reading early drafts and proposals, and supporting me through this journey to secure his future "stay at home dad" status (inside joke), thank you. You were as important to getting this book done as I was. Thank you for believing in me. For lifting me up with encouraging words when I was hard on myself. For reminding me of my vision, my purpose, and my spiritual gift. For the talks about finances (your expertise) and for being a guiding light in this journey. Thank you. I couldn't imagine having accomplished this without you. You're my biggest supporter and you give it to me straight. What an extraordinary combination. Your humor and love carry me through—always. I'm forever indebted to you.

To my siblings, for holding it down in the "trenches" together. Marilyn and Olany, you both have played a pivotal part in my life. Each of you provided me with just the inspiration I needed to take on life. You've individually provided me with the sisterhood I needed and didn't know it. I appreciate your feedback during this book process. Your confirmation and validation were exactly what I required to be bold enough to share this story. For the times we've all been aggravated with our mother's circumstances, no one knew better than you two about the realities we've faced. Forever indebted to you. To my brother, I pray God continues to guide you to sobriety that you may heal from the things which you don't speak of and that you feel whole and happy again.

To my nieces and nephews. Thank you for giving me another chance at motherhood with a twist. To my niece Yesmene, thank you for being such a bright star and being as excited about this story as I was. For your help with my website, your feedback, shared resources, and your unconditional support. You are truly another bright and shining star within our family and proof that we "old folk" can learn some things from this generation. Your love and dedication are sure to take you places you've never imagined. God has got his hands on you.

To my cousins, the saying couldn't be truer: "God made us cousins because he knew our mothers couldn't handle us as siblings." (author unknown) For the moments of happiness you provided in my childhood, adolescence, and adulthood, *thank you*. Because of you, I knew I always had great times to look forward to. Your support and your love don't go unnoticed.

To Stacey Dyer, for being the second mother I needed. You arrived in our lives at just the right time. And what's best is you gave us all the incomparable gift of Derrick, our now guardian angel. For the moments I needed some motherly advice, no one knew better than you how to best address my "only child" woes. Your calm and joyous demeanor reaches my heart every time. Thank you for loving our Cesar in the most amazing way. The best Granny ever. You gave me hope at a time when I felt hopeless. Your faith-driven spirit shows you are truly an angel on earth. The words "thank you" just don't cut it some days for all the goodness you've provided in our world.

To Giselle with Ready Writer Services LLC, you were right on time. I'm forever indebted to you for your editorial help, keen insight, and ongoing support in bringing my story to life.

For the days you were more than an editor, you were the "therapist" I needed to break me from my fear of vulnerability. You reminded me of the importance of sharing details that would connect with my readers, albeit difficult to re-explore. You, ma'am, are truly anointed. Thank you for your gentle but firm guidance, for teaching me the ways of this publishing world, and for always being a phone call away. Forever grateful.

To Jessica Cornelio, thank you for your feedback. For the final word, I needed to feel comfortable submitting this work. You were the icing on the cake. Your literary knowledge was just what I didn't know I needed to wrap up the manuscript that would become the book you have before you today.

To Terry Whalin, for giving me the opportunity to pitch the book. For the moment of fate you provided, before I even knew how God had led me to you. God placed me in just the right place, at just the right time, and led me to do just the right thing by reaching out to you about your book, *Book Proposals That Sell.* Little did I know a simple moment of gratitude on LinkedIn would lead me to the distinct opportunity to initiate my publishing journey with Morgan James Publishing. Grateful for your fighting for my book to be given the chance to see the bookshelves of many brick & mortar and online stores around the world so that I may share this message of hope with all the women who need it. Thank you.

To Pastor Sam, for inspiring me spiritually and personally. For showing support in even the most dire of circumstances. More than my pastor you've been a source of inspiration for our family. Your genuine show of care and concern throughout our difficult times helped me process those moments enough to be able to pen them on paper. For agreeing to support me in any way through the promotion of this book, and for your guiding hand. Beyond blessed to have you in our lives.

To Emily, my Morgan James Publishing Author Relations Manager, for rooting for me and making my concerns known through the production of this book. You saw my vision and steadfastly carried the word to the rest of the team. Producing what I now consider to be a true work of art. From the cover page to the interior layout and beyond. I'm forever grateful to you and the production team.

To my girlfriends, Damaris, Michelle, and Elizabeth, thank you for the push. For the nudge to finally get back to it. To the place that truly completed me. My writing. To share my story. Your words of encouragement and cheer-leading have not gone unnoticed. You were just what I needed in the moments I needed it. The brief escapes that gave me the energy to keep going. Friendships like these are hard to find. I consider it an honor to call you sisters.

And finally, to you, my reader. Writing a book is harder than I thought and more rewarding than I could have ever imagined. None of this would have been possible without the simple seed of a thought that all of you have also struggled or know someone who's struggled with overcoming failure. For the women who have struggled and are struggling in their mother-daughter relationships. The ones who found themselves hopeless in those moments in life where no hope could be seen. The women who have endured, persevered, and come out on top even amid the darkest moments of their lives. And those seeking to do better and be better. This book is for you.

Although this period of my life was filled with many ups and downs, writing a book about the story of my life is a surreal process. Having an idea and turning it into a book is as hard as it sounds. The experience is both internally challenging and rewarding. It is because of the aforementioned individuals' efforts and encouragement that I have a legacy to pass on to my family where one didn't exist before. Thank you!

ABOUT THE AUTHOR

Lin Green is a writer, advocate, blogger, and public speaker residing in Orlando, Florida. As a community advocate with a background in criminal justice, public administration, crisis intervention, and crisis counseling, Lin currently holds a long-standing position with a government agency spanning over fifteen years, under which she's also served as a volunteer working with children overseen by the Department of Children and Families. As the former program director for a mentoring program she co-developed for young ladies in Seminole County, FL, she's aware of the struggles that families in transition face. Lin speaks publicly on these issues at venues such as human trafficking conferences, the local Sheriff's Office Community Law Enforcement Academy, periodically at the University of Central Florida's local campus, and as needed in other community forums. Additionally, Lin has traveled to crisis incidents throughout the country to provide support as a member of the Florida Crisis Response Team. She's a member of her county's Domestic Violence Task Force as well as the Sexual Assault Response Team, and a Greater Orlando Human Trafficking Task Force (GOHTTF) liaison. Lin has been highlighted in *Orlando Voyager* magazine as a "Featured Change Maker."

ENDNOTES

1 von Reynolds, Shola. "Exploring the Concept of Beauty and its Fashion History." *Another.* July 14, 2016. https://www.anothermag.com/fashion-beauty/8861/exploring-the-concept-of-beauty-and-its-fashion-history.

2 Wikipedia. 2022. "May 1981." Wikimedia Foundation. Last modified August 21, 2022. https://en.wikipedia.org/wiki/May_1981.

3 Manley, Elizabeth S. "Revitalizing Feminism in the Dominican Republic." NACLA. November 27, 2018. https://nacla.org/news/2018/11/27/revitalizing-feminism-dominican-republic.

4 Wikipedia. 2023. "Dominican Republic Immigration to Puerto Rico." Wikimedia Foundation. Last modified August 21, 2023. https://en.wikipedia.org/wiki/Dominican_Republic_immigration_to_Puerto_Rico.

5 Wikipedia. 2023. "Childhood Amnesia." Wikimedia Foundation. Last modified May 11, 2023. https://en.wikipedia.org/wiki/Childhood_amnesia.

6   "What Is an Amniocentesis?" Johns Hopkins Medicine. The Johns Hopkins University, January 1, 2023. https://www.hopkinsmedicine.org/health/treatment-tests-and-therapies/amniocentesis#:~:text=Amniocentesis%20is%20a%20procedure%20used, Protects%20against%20infection.

7   "Anhidrosis (Lack of Sweat)." Cleveland Clinic. The Cleveland Clinic, April 19, 2021. https://my.cleveland clinic.org/health/diseases/15891-anhidrosis-lack-of-sweat.

8   Yen-Chin, Liu, Kuo Rei-Lin, and Shih Shin-Ru. "COVID-19: The First Documented Coronavirus Pandemic in History." Biomedical Journal, Volume 43, Issue 4. Science Direct, May 5, 2020. https://doi.org/10.1016/j.bj.2020.04.007.

9   Huber, Liz. "Why Limiting Beliefs Hold You Back in Life & What To Do About It." Medium. The StartUp, June 13, 2019. https://medium.com/swlh/why-limiting-beliefs-hold-you-back-in-life-what-to-do-about-it-e877f6e36bd2.

A free ebook edition is available with the purchase of this book.

To claim your free ebook edition:

1. Visit MorganJamesBOGO.com
2. Sign your name CLEARLY in the space
3. Complete the form and submit a photo of the entire copyright page
4. You or your friend can download the ebook to your preferred device

A **FREE** ebook edition is available for you or a friend with the purchase of this print book.

CLEARLY SIGN YOUR NAME ABOVE

Instructions to claim your free ebook edition:
1. Visit MorganJamesBOGO.com
2. Sign your name CLEARLY in the space above
3. Complete the form and submit a photo of this entire page
4. You or your friend can download the ebook to your preferred device

Print & Digital Together Forever.

Snap a photo

Free ebook

Read anywhere

Printed in the USA
CPSIA information can be obtained
at www.ICGtesting.com
JSHW020241060424
60652JS00002B/34